Return of the Red Heifers

PAVING THE ROAD TO REDEMPTION

Return of the Red Heifers

PAVING THE ROAD TO REDEMPTION

Adam Eliyahu Berkowitz

Table of Contents

Disclaimer

A S WILL BE explained, the red heifer has baffled sages for thousands of years. Every aspect of this enigmatic mitzvah (Torah commandment), indeed, every aspect of the Temple service, must be carried out with uncompromising precision and faithfulness. From approximately 1300 BCE, when the Jews received the Torah at Sinai, until 70 CE, the Temple service was carried out every day, except for the 70-year Babylonian exile. The myriad details of the Temple and its service are discussed at length in the Talmud and other Jewish sources.

Studying the Bible is not nearly enough. Understanding the Temple or its service requires a complete grasp of these sources, and few scholars today have such a grasp. This book is not intended as an authoritative source. While every effort has been made to research this vital subject carefully, the Temple Institute rabbis have studied the subject intensively for almost 40 years. The author believes they are the only scholars qualified to rule on these subjects. Any statements about the red heifer that do not meet their approval are categorically wrong.

Thanks

FIRST AND FOREMOST, I would like to thank the God of Israel who has faithfully kept his covenant and brought the Jews back from exile.

I would also like to thank Rabbi Tuly Weisz who hired me and tasked me with reporting on the unfolding process of redemption. His kindness and respect have changed my life. I believe his vision has changed the world.

I would like to thank Rabbi Elie Mischel whose faith in this project overcame all obstacles, including my own procrastination and reluctance.

I would also like to thank my wife whose inner aspect of *malchut* (nobility) channeled my light into the world.

Acknowledgments

I HAVE BEEN REPORTING on *geula* (redemption) from Israel for eight years. Eight Years ago, I was criticized and ridiculed for sensationalizing commonplace developments without significance. About three years ago, that criticism disappeared. It may have been COVID, which appeared like the hand of God and made many realize the human limitations of governments. It may have been the breakdown of governments worldwide and the threat of World War III.

These events forced people to respond. Some turned to God and community. A surprising number of Christians turned to Israel in love. Some chose to embrace radical Islam. While everyone chose a different path, it was undeniable that the world had changed and was about to change even more.

Through my reporting, it became clear that the Third Temple will characterize this change. While the arrival of the red heifers in Israel ignited world attention, it is far from being the most remarkable thing I have reported on. The Jewish people are much closer to reviving the Temple service than most people realize, though the preparations have gone largely unnoticed outside of a small circle of Jews. These Jews have been working quietly to bring back aspects of the Temple service that had not been seen for two millennia.

Their method and motivation was simple: God commanded us. We cannot choose, and we cannot abandon the Torah.

It must be understood that this move towards *geula* was not led by rabbis or the government of Israel. Indeed, these are some of the biggest obstacles left to overcome. After the IDF conquered the Temple Mount in the 1967 Six-Day War, Moshe Dayan returned control of Judaism's holiest site to Jordan. As the number of Jews visiting the Temple Mount grew exponentially, several prominent rabbis issued warnings that doing so violated Jewish law.

In 1967, a young soldier arrived at the Temple Mount. While the Israeli government rejected the vision of a return to Solomon's Temple, Rabbi Ariel established the Temple Institute to prepare the nation. His efforts produced meager results, and he was marginalized by the government and media, who labeled him a dangerous extremist.

But gradually, the nation woke up from the exile. Make no mistake, the Temple movement is grassroots. Young Haredim ignore the mandates of their rabbis and ascend to the Temple Mount. Mourning the destruction of the Temples on Tisha B'Av is close to being a festive holiday as young people dance around the walls of the Old City waving flags. The police are turning a blind eye to Jewish prayer, Jews prostrating on the holy stones, blowing the shofar, waving lulav. Many politicians have realized that a photo-op on the Temple Mount will garner votes.

And the Arabs have made it clear that land for peace won't bring peace because it is not the land they want.

There have been heroes in the movement. Rabbi Yisrael Ariel is undoubtedly one of them. I still tremble in his presence. He exudes holiness and a love of God and Israel. I remember watching him at one Temple event as young boys danced around him. I was getting a glimpse of what the Temple will be like.

Rabbi Yehudah Glick was labeled by the media as the "most dangerous man in the Middle East" and shot by an Arab. His crime? Advocating for the Temple Mount as a "House of Prayer for All Nations." Indeed, Rabbi Glick is the gentlest man I know and exudes kindness.

Rabbi Baruch Kahane, who trains *Kohanim* (priests) and frequently acts as the *Kohen Gadol* (High Priest) at Temple reenactments, is soft-spoken and performs his duty with a smile, just as I had always imagined Aaron the priest would.

Rabbi Azariah Ariel, Rabbi Yisrael's son, oversees the Red Heifer project. While I am far from a scholar, he considers my questions seriously. I am assured that when the red heifer ceremony is performed, he will ensure it is precisely as the sages would have wanted. There will be no compromises.

Yes, the Nation of Israel is waking up from the 2,000-year dream of exile. In exile, Jews were "a nation that dwells alone." However, the First Temple was built with the help of Hiram of Lebanon, and the Second Temple was built with the help of Cyrus. Love of the God of Israel is not exclusive to Jews. The Temple is a house of prayer for all nations where all of mankind comes together to serve God. It transcends religion, race, and nationality.

The Third Temple is inevitable. This is a great comfort for some, those who hope our troubled world can come together and heal. Those who prefer a world without the most significant physical reminder that God rules the world are fighting this.

But it will happen, and God will be willing, very soon. The Nation of Israel has waited long enough.

Prologue

Migdal Eder, Judea, 3738, 23 BCE

THE OIL LAMP sputtered as Ephraim rose from his sleeping mat, careful not to wake Rachel and their newborn son. The pre-dawn air held autumn's first bite, and he pulled his woolen cloak tight around his shoulders. He could see the stars still bright over the Judean hills through the window, though they would soon fade as the sun rose over the distant Dead Sea. He packed his phylacteries in a small cloth sack and slipped his four-cornered garment over his head, but it was still too early to say the morning prayers.

His daughter Chana was already awake, baking some flatbreads in a pan of sizzling oil. She doted on her father and always packed food for him when he traveled. She was almost a woman, and several of his kinsmen had already suggested that their sons be her husband. She would accompany him to Jerusalem. Just a few weeks ago, she had spent all the intermediary days of the Feast of Tabernacles dancing in the Temple at the festive water-libation ceremony celebrations.

His young donkey shifted restlessly in the courtyard, sensing the upcoming journey. Ephraim checked the ropes securing the woven basket that held two turtledoves—his voluntary burnt offering. He was careful to handle them in a way that would not transfer impurity. The birds cooed softly as he adjusted their covering.

He reflected on previous years when the only voluntary offering he could afford was a grain offering. For now, a pair of birds was all he could afford as a carpenter of modest means but it would certainly help him feel closer to God. Not everyone could bring a lamb or goat to the Temple, but the Law provided for all levels of means, and his gratitude to *Hashem* was no less profound for the humbleness of his offering. They had been praying for a son for several years, and their prayers were finally answered. He felt overwhelming gratitude and wanted to bring a sacrifice to the Temple to express this.

Rachel appeared in the doorway, wrapping a shawl around her shoulders.

"Remember that you have to be purified," she said. Ephraim nodded. His son would be named for Rachel's father, who passed away just before the holiday. Ephraim had helped prepare him for burial. It was a powerful commandment but brought with it the necessity to be sprinkled with the ashes of the red heifer. It was an inconvenience but one Ephraim was happy to endure. His father-in-law had been an especially righteous man, and Ephraim hoped that in the merit of the commandment and by giving his name to his son, his father-in-law's righteousness would influence his son's life.

He led the donkey past his neighbors' huts in Migdal Eder, past shuttered homes and workshops. The only sounds were his sandals on the packed earth and the soft clip of the donkey's hooves. They were traveling light, as Jerusalem was only a few hours away. Ephraim knew the way, and the Path of the Patriarchs was clearly marked, making it easy to follow even before sunrise. At the village well, he met Shimon, the potter, who would join him for the journey. Travelers had been using this road for centuries, and traveling together was more pleasant and safer than traveling alone. Roman rule had many disadvantages, but it meant that there were fewer bandits these days.

As they set out on the familiar path, the eastern sky lightened, reaching the pre-dawn stage the sages called 'the pillar of dawn.' Ephraim recited the *Shema* prayer under his breath—the ancient declaration of Jewish faith proclaiming the oneness of God—emphasizing the phrase, "When you are walking on your way" (Deuteronomy 6:7). He added the words of King David from Psalm 66: "I will enter Your house with burnt offerings; I will fulfill my vows to You." The words came unbidden to his lips, as natural as breathing. How many generations of his forefathers had made this same journey, their hearts full of thanksgiving?

The road wound through terraced hillsides heavy with ripening olives. Here and there, workers were already out with their long poles, beginning the harvest. The morning light caught the silver undersides of the leaves as they stirred in the breeze. Ephraim remembered his father telling him how King David himself might have walked this very path, ascending to Jerusalem with songs of praise.

As the sun cleared the horizon, they rounded a bend, and there it was—Jerusalem, gleaming like a pearl in the morning light. The massive walls rose proud and strong, but it was the Temple that drew every eye. Herod's masterwork dominated the city, its white limestone and gold ornamentation catching the sun's rays. Even after seeing it countless times, the sight still filled Ephraim with awe.

They joined the stream of pilgrims flowing through the city gates. It was the second day of the week, a market day, and the streets grew more crowded as they approached the Temple Mount. Merchants were setting up their stalls; priests were hurrying to their duties; other families were bringing their offerings. The babel of voices speaking Hebrew, Aramaic, and Greek filled the air, along with the scents of incense and cooking fires.

As he approached the Pilgrims' Road that ascended to the Temple, Ephraim turned towards the Mount of Olives. He needed to be purified from his contact with the dead body. The ritual purification was complex and ancient. The ashes of the red heifer were essential for cleansing those who had come into contact with death, allowing them to be restored to ritual purity. Ephraim knew the process well—a perfect, unblemished red heifer had been sacrificed outside the city, and its ashes mixed with living water. A priest would use hyssop to sprinkle this mixture on anyone who had touched a corpse as Ephraim had when preparing his father-in-law for burial. It was a paradoxical ritual: the same mixture that purified it also rendered the priests who prepared it temporarily impure. The intricacies of the law never ceased to humble him.

Ephraim climbed the Mount of Olives, entering the subterranean chamber and waiting until it was full of people. He had been here just a few days ago for the first sprinkling of the water mixed with the red heifer ashes, and this sprinkling would complete the process. The priest entered, a bunch of hyssop clutched in his hand. He took the lid off a large cask of water that stood ready next to a low platform. He stepped up, dipping the hyssop into the cask, before waving it briskly toward the people. Ephraim felt several drops of water hit his face. The door was opened and the people began to exit. Another door led to an underground ritual bath for the men. Ephraim disrobed quickly and immersed, putting on his clothes while he was still damp and shivering. He hurried to the Temple, eager to bring his offering.

At the Temple steps, Ephraim handed Shimon the donkey's lead and lifted the turtle dove's basket. His heart quickened as he ascended. Soon, he would stand in the Court of Israel, watching the smoke of his offering rise toward heaven. Soon, he would speak the ancient words of blessing, adding his voice to the endless chain of fathers thanking the Holy One for the gift of a son.

At the Court of the Priests, a Levite approached him. Ephraim carefully lifted the basket of turtle doves, presenting them to the priest who would perform the sacrifice. The priest examined the birds carefully, ensuring they were without blemish. With practiced hands, he took the first bird, nipping the nape of its neck with his long thumbnail before draining its blood into a consecrated vessel. The precise movements were unchanged from the days of his ancestors—a continuity that connected the priest to generations past. The bird's body was then salted and placed upon the altar's fire, its smoke rising heavenward as a pleasing aroma to the Holy One. For Ephraim, this was more than ritual—it was a profound expression of his love of God and connected him to the living chain of ancestors stretching back to the patriarchs.

The process was repeated for the second bird and smoke filled his nostrils as the wind shifted. The smell of burning meat was a powerful reminder of a lifetime marked by devotion to God's service.

The morning sun now blazed full on the Temple's walls, and the glare nearly blinded him for a moment. When his vision cleared, Ephraim paused, overwhelmed by a sudden wave of emotion. Here he stood, where his father had stood, and his father's father before him, giving thanks for the new life granted by the God of Israel. In a few days, he would bring his son for circumcision, welcoming him into the covenant. For now, though, he simply breathed in the sanctity of the moment, his heart full of gratitude for the precious child entrusted to his care.

Introduction

THE JEWISH PEOPLE'S connection to the Temple in Jerusalem has been unbreakable throughout history. Even during the long and dark exile, Jews never abandoned their hope of returning to Jerusalem and rebuilding the Temple. Three times daily, Jews face Jerusalem in prayer, beseeching God to "return in mercy to Jerusalem Your city and dwell therein as You have promised." After every meal, Jews pray for the rebuilding of "Jerusalem, the holy city, speedily in our days." At every wedding, the groom breaks a glass to remember the destruction of the Temple, declaring, "If I forget you, O Jerusalem, let my right hand forget its skill" (Psalms 137:5).

This devotion to the Temple spans three millennia of Jewish history. When the First Temple, built by King Solomon, was destroyed by the Babylonians in 586 BCE, the Jewish people maintained their faith through 70 years of exile. The prophet Ezekiel, himself in exile in Babylon, received detailed visions of the future Temple (Ezekiel 40-48). When Cyrus the Great permitted the Jews to return to Jerusalem, they immediately began rebuilding the Temple, completing it in 516 BCE despite fierce opposition from neighboring peoples.

The Second Temple stood for over 500 years before its destruction by the Romans in 70 CE. This loss was catastrophic for the Jewish people, yet they never abandoned hope. The

Talmud records that even as the Temple burned, new Jewish legal academies were established to preserve Torah knowledge for future generations. Throughout nearly two millennia of exile, Jews preserved the laws and customs related to the Temple, studying them in detail and incorporating them into their prayers despite their seeming irrelevance to daily life.

The return of the Jewish people to the land of Israel over the last 150 years was transformative for Jewish religious life. Jewish legal issues that were not practically relevant for 2,000 years, such as the Sabbatical year (*shemittah*), suddenly became living and breathing applicable laws once again. The Jewish people revived biblical commandments that hadn't been performed since the Second Temple burned.

When Jerusalem was liberated and unified in 1967, rebuilding the Temple suddenly seemed within reach. On that fateful day, when Israeli soldiers heroically fought their way through the streets of the Old City of Jerusalem, Rabbi Yisrael Ariel was among the first soldiers to reach the Temple Mount, the holiest site for the Jews. Assigned by his officer to guard the site while his IDF unit advanced to take the Western Wall - essentially a retaining wall for the first and second Temples - Rabbi Yisrael felt that his life would never be the same.

The prophets had foretold this return in vivid detail. Isaiah proclaimed, "And it shall come to pass in the end of days, that the mountain of the Lord's house shall be established as the top of the mountains, and shall be exalted above the hills; and all nations shall flow unto it" (Isaiah 2:2). Zechariah described a time when "There shall yet be old men and old women sitting in the squares of Jerusalem" (Zechariah 8:4), a scene now visible daily in the restored Jewish capital.

After the war, Rabbi Ariel founded the Temple Institute to advance the study of the Temple and its service, with the ultimate goal of rebuilding the Temple and reinstating its service.

Toward this end, the Temple Institute has reconstructed the Temple utensils and musical instruments, the priestly garments, and even the seven-branched golden candelabrum (*Menorah*). Levites and *Kohanim,* the priestly descendants of Aaron, stand ready to take their role in the Temple.

The Institute's work reflects a broader awakening of interest in Temple studies throughout Israeli society. What was once the domain of a small group of scholars has become a subject of widespread fascination. Religious schools now include detailed Temple studies in their curriculum. Advanced programs train priests in the intricate laws of the Temple service. The number of Jews visiting the Temple Mount has grown exponentially - from just a few thousand annually in the early 2000s to over 50,000 in 2023 alone.

But this surge of religious fervor exists within a complex political and diplomatic framework. After the liberation of the Temple Mount in 1967, Defense Minister Moshe Dayan made the controversial decision to remove the Israeli flag and to return Judaism's holiest site to the administrative control of the Islamic Waqf while Israel maintained security control. Jewish activity at the site was limited by the "status quo" based on a firman (decree) of Ottoman sultan Osman III in 1757 that preserved the division of ownership and responsibilities of Jerusalem's holy sites. While the "status quo" ensured Muslim dominance, it violated Israeli law which mandates equality of religion. Despite this contradiction, the "status quo" has been maintained by successive Israeli governments in the face of growing calls for change. Under current rules, Jews are permitted to visit the Temple Mount during limited hours. Jews may not visit at night or on Shabbat and are barred from entering on Muslim holidays. While Muslims are free to pray, this right is withheld from Jews - a restriction that many view as a violation of fundamental religious rights. Indeed, Jews may not wear phylacteries, bring holy books onto the site, or perform any religious rituals such as blowing the ram's horn on *Rosh Hashanah* (Jewish New Year) or waving the four species on the Feast of Tabernacles.

Despite these political constraints, religious preparations for the Temple's restoration continue unabated. While changes to the status quo would require complex diplomatic negotiations and unprecedented political agreements, the Temple Institute and other organizations focus on the aspects within their control: training priests, recreating vessels, and preparing for the religious requirements of Temple service. Among these requirements, one of the most challenging has been incredibly elusive: a red heifer. This supremely rare sacrifice is necessary for the purification ritual described in Numbers 19. The sages record that only nine red heifers were prepared from the time of Moses until the destruction of the Second Temple. During the Middle Ages, Maimonides noted that the Messiah would prepare the tenth red heifer. Nevertheless, various Jewish communities have searched for potential red heifers throughout history. In the 1990s, several candidates were identified but ultimately disqualified due to the exceedingly stringent requirements.

Then, in Septermber, 2022 five red calves were discovered in Texas and brought to Israel to reinstate this biblical commandment. The Temple Institute's leadership understood that if this inexplicable and rare commandment could be reinstated, the nation could be purified, and the full Temple service could be re-established.

Few events have captured the attention of so many people around the world. As a journalist for Israel365 News, I had the honor of breaking this extraordinary story - which became our most widely-read article in several years. Due to my long experience of writing stories about the unfolding redemption taking place in Israel, I was chosen by the organizers to be the only journalist at Ben Gurion Airport when the heifers arrived. Work at the busy freight terminal stopped as the large pen holding the young heifers was unloaded. Even the terminal workers, mostly non-religious, knew something historic was happening.

News spread rapidly across global media outlets and social networks, resonating deeply with audiences worldwide. The story touched deep religious and historical chords that transcended cultural boundaries. For Jews, it represented another step toward the fulfillment of ancient prophecies. For many Christians, particularly those who study end-times prophecies, it signaled the potential approach of messianic times. The import was clear even to the most skeptical atheists.

Yet perhaps the most revealing reaction came from jihadist Muslims dedicated to Israel's destruction. In the wake of Hamas' brutal October 7 attack on Israel and the war that followed, both Hamas and Hezbollah explicitly connected their actions to these red heifers. On the 100th day of the war, which Hamas named the Al-Aqsa Flood, a Hamas spokesman cited the arrival of the red heifers as a primary reason for their attack, claiming it signaled the imminent construction of the third Temple predicted by biblical prophets. Shortly afterward, Hezbollah threatened to attack an Israeli conference discussing the religious commandment of the red heifer. IDF soldiers returning from Gaza reported finding images of the Temple Mount's golden-domed shrine in every home they entered, underscoring that the goal of the Al-Aqsa Flood was to maintain Muslim control of the sacred site and prevent any possibility of rebuilding the Temple.

These violent reactions, however, fundamentally misunderstand both Jewish intentions and religious requirements. While the arrival of red heifers might indeed signal messianic times drawing closer, this doesn't translate to imminent plans to alter the current arrangement at the holy site. The red heifer ceremony itself must be performed on the Mount of Olives, not the Temple Mount, and can be conducted without affecting the status quo. Furthermore, even a revival of Temple sacrifices could potentially be carried out using a temporary altar without disturbing existing Muslim structures.

While the Temple in Jerusalem has always remained central to Jewish identity, referenced in daily prayers and maintained as a cherished dream, Israel has consistently maintained Muslim access and administration of the site for 57 years, even though it could have chosen a different path. Yet media outlets have often adopted an Islamist narrative, falsely accusing Israel of planning to seize the compound and destroy Al-Aqsa, despite Israel's proven track record of preserving Muslim religious rights.

While the arrival of the red heifers has indeed brought the possibility of reinstating certain Temple rituals closer to reality, this does not necessarily mean changing the current arrangements at Judaism's holiest site.

While Muslim reactions focused on fears of immediate Temple construction, some Christians adopted a different but equally mistaken theology stating that the ashes of the red heifer would usher in the "Temple of the Antichrist", a version of Christian eschatology in which a false Messiah will use the rebuilt Temple to declare himself to humanity. This interpretation ignores the numerous biblical prophecies about the restoration of Temple worship. The prophet Ezekiel provided detailed blueprints for the future Temple (Ezekiel 40-48). Jeremiah proclaimed that Jerusalem would be "rebuilt upon its ruins, and the Temple will be restored to its proper service" (Jeremiah 30:18). Isaiah envisioned a time when "My house shall be called a house of prayer for all peoples" (Isaiah 56:7).

Resolution is inevitable; the day will come when the Temple will be rebuilt. The same prophets who promised that God would return the Jews to Israel also promised that the Temple in Jerusalem would be built, never to be destroyed again. In the meantime, as servants of God, Jews perform the commandments without question. The Bible commands us to prepare a red heifer, so we do our absolute best to carry out God's will as expressed in the Torah, regardless of political considerations.

My grandfather grew up in a world without Jewish independence in Israel. My father grew up in a world without a unified Jerusalem. I pray that my children will see a world in which God's glory is revealed in His Temple. We have merited to live in a generation in which biblical prophecies are manifest before our eyes. God has returned the Jewish people to the promised land. The deserts are blooming. And if we remain faithful to our covenant, we will soon merit returning to the Temple Mount and rebuilding the Temple, the House of Prayer for all nations.

CHAPTER ONE

Red Heifer: The Most Enigmatic Commandment

SOME RELIGIOUS COMMANDMENTS seem logical and straightforward - honor your parents, don't steal, don't murder. Others require interpretation but we can suggest meaningful reasons for keeping them - keeping kosher promotes mindful eating, the Sabbath provides essential rest. But one commandment has puzzled Jewish scholars for thousands of years, challenging human understanding and becoming the very symbol of divine wisdom that transcends human logic: the ritual of the red heifer. Yet this ancient purification ritual, with its complex requirements and apparent contradictions, remains central to Temple service and ritual purity even in modern times.

The Mystery of the Red Heifer

Despite its seemingly straightforward biblical description, the commandment of the red heifer is considered the most enigmatic of all 613 biblical commandments. Ancient Jewish sages classified it as the quintessential *chok*—a divine decree that defies human logic and must be accepted purely on faith. Even King Solomon, renowned as the wisest of all men, reportedly declared about this commandment, "I thought I could fathom it, but it remains elusive" (Ecclesiastes 7:23).

What makes this commandment so mysterious? At its core, the red heifer ceremony appears to contradict itself in ways that challenge our understanding of ritual purity and impurity. Here are some of the paradoxes that have puzzled scholars for millennia:

The Location Paradox

Once the Temple in Jerusalem was constructed, sacrifices could only be offered at that site. Temple offerings must be brought inside the Temple complex, following strict rules about where each type of sacrifice can be performed. Yet the preparation of the red heifer takes place entirely outside the Temple - specifically on the Mount of Olives, facing the Temple's entrance but separated from it by the Kidron Valley. While removing a sacrifice from the Temple area would normally render it unfit, the red heifer ceremony and the equally enigmatic *Yom Kippur* (Day of Atonement) "scapegoat" are the only sacrifice-like rituals that are performed outside the Temple. Rather than being burned on the altar, the red heifer is burned atop a pyre, the wood becoming an element of the sacrifice. This departure from normal sacrificial procedure raises profound questions about the nature of the red heifer. While the red heifer is used to purify and not as an offering, it is referred to as a *chatat* (sin offering).

The Designation Paradox

Since becoming ritually impure is not considered a sin, the designation of the red heifer as a *chatat* seems paradoxical. However, this terminology suggests a deeper parallel. Just as sin creates a spiritual barrier that makes one unfit to approach God until he brings a sin offering, ritual impurity likewise creates a barrier to approaching God. The red heifer ceremony is like a sin offering in the sense that it restores the person's ability to come close in service to God.

The Purification Paradox

The most striking contradiction involves the priests who prepare the ashes of the red heifer. These ashes, used to purify others, render the priests who prepare them ritually impure. It is a profound paradox - the very substance that cleanses one person defiles another. This mysterious duality stands as one of the deepest enigmas of this divine commandment.

The Burning Paradox

Unlike other sacrifices, where specific parts of the animal are burned on the altar and other parts are either eaten by the priests or disposed of in prescribed ways, the red heifer is burned in its entirety - hide, flesh, blood, and even its dung. Nothing is separated or removed. This complete consumption by fire sets it apart from every other Temple offering.

Why It Matters Today

You might wonder why an ancient purification ritual is so important in the modern world. The answer lies in understanding the concept of ritual impurity and its implications for Jewish life and the Temple service.

Understanding Ritual Impurity

First, it's essential to understand that ritual impurity is not about physical cleanliness or moral status. A perfectly righteous person can be ritually impure, and a wicked person can be ritually pure. Ritual impurity is a spiritual state that affects one's ability to participate in the Temple service and interact with sacred objects.

The most severe form of ritual impurity comes from contact with or proximity to a dead body. The details of this aspect of Jewish law will be discussed in a later chapter. This impurity, called *tumat met*, can only be removed through a specific process involving the ashes of the red heifer. Without these ashes, the impurity remains.

The Current Situation

The elements needed for the red heifer ceremony have been lacking since the destruction of the Second Temple in 70 CE. There has been no red heifer, no scarlet dye, nor any kosher priests. For nearly two millennia, Jews lacked sovereignty in their ancestral land, further preventing any preparations to restore this Temple service. As a result, every Jew today is considered ritually impure from ancestral contact with the dead. Therefore, while we can begin preparations for the Third Temple, even if the Temple were to be built tomorrow, significant limitations on restoring the complete Temple service remain.

However, this doesn't mean that all Temple services are impossible. Jewish law makes essential distinctions:

What Can Be Done Without the Red Heifer

- Time-bound public services can be performed even in a state of ritual impurity if necessary. This includes:
  - The twice-daily eternal sacrifice (*korban tamid*)
  - The additional offerings for Sabbath and festivals (*musafim*)
  - The Paschal lamb sacrifice
- These services are so important that they override the normal requirements for ritual purity.

What Requires the Red Heifer

- Personal, non-time-dependent sacrifices cannot be brought without purification through the red heifer ashes. These include:
  - Sin offerings (*chatat*)
  - Guilt offerings (*asham*)
  - Peace offerings (*shelamim*)
  - Thanksgiving offerings

- Handling and consumption of sacred foods is also restricted, including:
  - First fruits (*bikurim*)
  - Fourth-year fruit (*neta revai*)
  - Various tithes (*terumah*, *ma'aser*, and *challah*)

International Implications

The impact of this ritual extends beyond the Jewish people. Throughout history, non-Jews have brought offerings to the Temple in Jerusalem, following the prophet Isaiah's vision of the Temple as a "house of prayer for all nations" (Isaiah 56:7). King Solomon himself, in his dedication speech after the completion of the First Temple, prays that God should grant the requests of all people who pray at the Temple, Jews and non-Jews alike (I Kings 8:41-43). While non-Jews did not participate in the public sacrifices, they could bring personal offerings. However, without the ashes of the red heifer, there are no Jewish priests who are currently in the state of purity required to perform these services on behalf of anyone, Jewish or non-Jewish.

The Deeper Meaning

Jewish scholars have long suggested that the very incomprehensibility of the red heifer commandment carries profound spiritual lessons. It teaches humility before divine wisdom and reminds us that not everything in our relationship with God needs to be fully understood to be meaningful and true. Just as a child may not understand why certain medicines taste bitter but still benefit from them, we may not comprehend the reason for every divine commandment but can still benefit from their observance. The red heifer reminds us that divine wisdom often transcends human logic, and that faith sometimes requires us to act even when we don't fully understand.

The paradoxes within the red heifer ritual - particularly how it purifies the impure while making the pure impure - also remind us that life itself is full of apparent contradictions that ultimately serve a higher purpose. Sometimes the process of helping others requires personal sacrifice, and what appears harmful in one context might be healing in another.

CHAPTER TWO

The Biblical Basics: Understanding The Red Heifer's Requirements

The Biblical Source

The Torah presents the commandment of the red heifer in characteristically concise language:

> *"This is the ritual law that the Lord has commanded: Instruct the children of Israel to bring you a perfectly red cow without blemish, in which there is no defect and on which no yoke has been laid."* (Numbers 19:2)

At first glance, these requirements seem straightforward – find a red cow that's never been used for work and has no physical defects. However, as with many biblical commandments, the oral tradition passed down through generations of Jewish scholars reveals layers of complexity that make finding a suitable red heifer one of the most challenging tasks in Jewish law.

The Age Requirement: More Than Just A Calf

The Hebrew words for "red cow," *para aduma*, are often trans-lated as "red heifer," which is misleading. The Hebrew word *"para"* specifically refers to a mature female cow, not a young calf. This distinction is crucial for understanding the age requirements. According to Jewish law, the animal must be at least two years and one day old to qualify for the ceremony. Before reaching two years of age, the animal is called an *"egla"* (calf), and only after passing this milestone does it become a *"para"* (cow).

Interestingly, while Jewish law sets a minimum age require-ment, it sets no maximum age limit - a mature cow remains eligible for the ceremony regardless of age. However, when the Temple stood in Jerusalem, age was rarely a practical concern since red heifers were prepared as soon as they reached the qualifying age to avoid any risk of disqualification. This age re-quirement directly affects the purchase protocol. Unlike other Temple-related items, the animal cannot be purchased as a calf with plans to raise it for its ashes. Instead, it must be bought with Temple funds only after reaching maturity. Until then, private owners must raise it under careful rabbinic supervision.

The Color Requirement: Perfectly Red

The Hebrew word *adumah* (red) in this context requires careful interpretation: it refers not to a bright crimson but rather to a shade of deep brown-red—a natural, earthen tone. The word *temima* (perfect) modifies the color requirement, demanding an extraordinary level of uniformity in the ani-mal's coloring.

Jewish tradition interprets "perfectly red" to mean that no more than one non-red hair is permitted on the entire body of the cow.[1] Even two adjacent non-red hairs would disqualify the animal. This color must be natural, not artificially induced,

---

1   Maimonides, Laws of the Red Heifer 1:2

making the search even more challenging.

The inspection process for verifying the color is rigorous and ongoing. Rabbis must examine every hair with magnifying glasses, beginning with an initial inspection one week after birth. However, certification at birth doesn't guarantee permanent qualification. The status of a potential red heifer can change over time - a perfect candidate might develop disqualifying hairs, while an imperfect candidate could become qualified if non-red hairs fall out naturally. This dynamic nature of qualification necessitates regular monitoring throughout the animal's life.

The Physical Perfection Requirement

The requirement for physical perfection extends far beyond color. The phrase "without blemish" demands complete physical integrity - no defects of any kind are permitted. The animal must be born through natural birth (not Caesarean section), maintain perfect health throughout its life, and remain free from even minor blemishes that might be acceptable for other Temple services.

This standard of perfection must be maintained throughout the animal's life. Any injury, illness, or genetic abnormality that develops would immediately disqualify the heifer. Even conditions that wouldn't impact the animal's health or function could render it unsuitable for this sacred purpose.

The Work Prohibition: "No Yoke"

Perhaps the most stringent requirement is the prohibition against work. The biblical phrase "no yoke has been laid" extends far beyond simply avoiding agricultural labor. According to Jewish law, the heifer must never have been used for any purpose whatsoever. This includes obvious forms of work like pulling loads or wearing a harness but also extends to seemingly minor activities like being leaned on or having items placed on its back.

Even allowing the animal to be mounted by a bull for breeding is prohibited, as bearing the bull's weight is considered a form of work. Inspectors must check for any signs of past use - bent or rubbed neck hairs that could indicate a yoke had been placed on its neck, calluses, worn areas, or changes in muscle development that might suggest the animal has been used for labor.

The Historical Context

Throughout history, only nine red heifers were prepared. The first was prepared by Moses himself in the wilderness, the second by Ezra after the return from Babylonian exile, and seven more during the Second Temple period. This historical record underscores the rarity and significance of finding suitable red heifers in our time. The fact that so few were found even during periods when the Temple stood and the search was actively pursued demonstrates the exceptional nature of this commandment.

Finding a red heifer in today's world presents unique challenges. Modern farming practices often involve using cattle at a young age, and most are bred for specific purposes from birth. Industrial farming methods can inadvertently create disqualifying conditions, and the need for constant supervision from birth makes the search even more complex. Authorities require ear tags and branding, both of which constitute blemishes that disqualify calves from the ceremony. The combination of perfect coloring, unblemished physical condition, and a complete absence of use makes finding a suitable red heifer one of the rarest occurrences in Jewish ritual life.

The exacting requirements for the red heifer remind us that divine service calls us to rise to extraordinary standards of precision and dedication. Each requirement, though demanding, elevates this ordinary animal to an instrument of profound spiritual significance. In the search for the red heifer, we find a powerful metaphor for the pursuit of holiness itself—a path that requires our fullest devotion and attention to detail, yet one where even a rare and carefully prepared offering can purify an entire community. Through these precise requirements, we learn that while the standards are high, they serve a profound purpose in transforming the mundane into the sacred.

Just as the red heifer preparation demands unwavering precision and a striving toward perfection, our own devotion to the particulars of spiritual practice—whether in prayer, study, or acts of kindness—can elevate everyday moments into opportunities for profound connection.

CHAPTER THREE

The Crimson Wool: A Sacred Dye Rediscovered

The Biblical Requirement

The Bible's instructions for the red heifer ceremony include a seemingly minor but crucial detail. Among the ingredients that must be burned with the red heifer, we find an intriguing requirement:

> "The priest shall take a piece of cedar wood, hyssop, and tolaat shani, and cast them into the burning of the cow" (Numbers 19:6)

This *tolaat shani*, traditionally translated as "crimson wool," represents one of the most fascinating elements of ancient Temple practice - a sacred dye whose secrets were lost to time, only to be rediscovered in our generation.

The Significance of Sacred Colors

In the ancient world, certain colors carried immense significance, both practical and spiritual. The Bible mentions the crimson dye twenty-five times, often in conjunction with two other precious colors: *tekhelet* (a sacred blue) and *argaman* (royal purple). These three colors represented the height of ancient textile craft and were reserved for the most prestigious uses.

The significance of these colors extended far beyond mere aesthetics. In the Temple, they adorned the sacred vestments worn by the priests and decorated the elaborate textiles that adorned the Tabernacle and later the Temple. The crimson, in particular, carried deep spiritual symbolism that would become central to several Temple rituals.

The Source of the Sacred Dye

The term *tolaat shani* contains a fascinating linguistic puzzle. While often translated as "crimson wool," the word *tolaat* actually refers not to the wool itself but to the tiny insect from which the dye is extracted. This creature, known scientifically as Kermes biblicus and called the "crimson worm" in rabbinic literature, produces one of the most precious natural dyes that was known to the ancient world.

The process of obtaining this dye reveals the extraordinary precision required in Temple-related matters. The female Kermes insects can only be found on the branches of a specific oak tree - Quercus ithaburensis - and only in certain regions of Israel. Even more remarkably, they are only available for collection during a brief two-week window in early spring.

During this period, the female insects attach their egg sacs to the tree branches, filling them with bright red eggs. Finding these tiny sacs requires keen eyes and patient dedication, as they're naturally camouflaged against the tree bark. The harvest is painstaking work; the yield is precious little dye from many insects.

The Rediscovery

For nearly two millennia, the exact identity of this biblical insect remained a matter of scholarly debate. The breakthrough came in 2002 when Dr. Zohar Amar of Bar Ilan University conducted groundbreaking research to identify the specific species mentioned in ancient texts. His work not only confirmed the identity of the Kermes biblicus but also succeeded in extracting the precious dye. However, his initial results suggested the color was more orange than the traditional understanding of crimson.

The Temple Institute, the leading authority on practical Temple-related research, eventually confirmed Dr. Amar's findings. This validation marked a crucial step toward reinstating this ancient practice.

The Dying Process

In 2022, a practical demonstration of the ancient dying process provided new insights into this lost art. Rabbi Yehoshua Friedman, dean of the Mikdash Yeshiva (a Torah institute focusing on Temple studies) and himself a Nazirite with the traditionally long hair this vow requires, demonstrated the intricate process of preparing the dye.

The procedure begins with a careful preparation of the dye bath. Alum, a mineral that serves as a mordant to help the dye bond with the wool, is dissolved in boiling water. The collected insect eggs are then immersed in this solution, where the alum serves two crucial functions: it helps set the dye and intensifies the resulting crimson color.

The wool must be immersed all at once - a requirement of Jewish law that ensures the entire piece receives the dye's initial and most potent effect. The wool remains in the solution for approximately an hour, during which time the dye penetrates the fibers. The insects remain in contact with the wool throughout this process, as straining them out prematurely might diminish the dye's effectiveness.

Modern Revival

The revival of this ancient craft has found a champion in Orna Hirshberg, a resident of Itamar in Samaria. Working under the guidance of the Temple Institute, she has dedicated herself to mastering this sacred art, understanding that it represents far more than just a historical curiosity - it's a crucial component for future Temple service.

The implications of this revival extend far beyond the red heifer ceremony. The crimson dye was integral to numerous Temple-related elements:

- The *ephod* (a special vestment of the High Priest)
- The sash worn by regular priests
- Various Temple tapestries
- The purification ritual for those afflicted with leprosy

Spiritual Symbolism

Perhaps the most profound use of the crimson wool was in the *Yom Kippur* (Day of Atonement) service, where it served as a powerful symbol of divine forgiveness. As described by the sages, a length of this crimson wool (known as the Scarlet-Dyed Tongue of Wool) played a crucial role in the dramatic ceremony of the scapegoat.

The ritual involved tying the crimson wool to both the Temple doors and the horns of the goat destined for Azazel. When the goat was cast off the cliff as part of the atonement ceremony, tradition holds that the crimson thread would miraculously turn white if God had accepted Israel's repentance. This transformation directly reflected the powerful words of the prophet Isaiah:

> "Come, let us reach an understanding — says the Lord. Be your sins like crimson, they can turn snow-white; Be they red as dyed wool, they can become like fleece" (Isaiah 1:18)

While the red heifer ceremony itself is neither a sacrifice nor a sin offering, the inclusion of crimson wool in its preparation creates a subtle link to this theme of purification and renewal. The transformation of color - from deep red to pure white - serves as a powerful metaphor for spiritual transformation and divine purification.

The rediscovery of this ancient dye in our time carries profound significance. Like many other aspects of Temple service being recovered in modern Israel, it represents another piece falling into place, another step toward the potential restoration of full Temple service. The fact that such discoveries are happening in our generation adds another layer to the remarkable story of Jewish return and renewal in the Holy Land.

CHAPTER FOUR

Preparing The Ashes: A Sacred Ritual Of Extraordinary Precision

The Priest's Preparation

The preparation of the red heifer's ashes represents one of the most intricate and carefully orchestrated ceremonies in Temple service. The ritual's complexity reflects its profound spiritual significance and the extraordinary measures required to maintain ritual purity throughout the process.

Much like the High Priest's preparation for the *Yom Kippur* (Day of Atonement) service, the priest chosen to perform the red heifer ceremony underwent an intensive period of isolation. Seven days before the ceremony, he would separate completely from his family, including his wife. This separation marked the beginning of an extraordinary spiritual journey that would culminate in the creation of the purifying ashes.

During this week of preparation, the priest lived in a unique chamber in the northeast corner of the Temple complex, known as "the chamber of stone." The choice of stone for this chamber was deliberate and significant — according to Jewish law, stone cannot receive ritual impurity, unlike materials such as wood or metal. Every aspect of the priest's environment during this crucial week was designed to maintain the highest possible level of ritual purity.

Throughout his week of seclusion, the priest underwent daily sprinklings with water containing ashes from a previous red heifer. This practice served as an additional safeguard, ensuring that any potential impurity from prior contact with the dead would be nullified. The attention to detail in these preparatory steps underscores the paramount importance of maintaining ritual purity throughout the ceremony.

The Day of the Ceremony

When the appointed day arrived, the atmosphere in Jerusalem was charged with anticipation. The ceremony began with a solemn procession. The elders of the *Sanhedrin* (the supreme Jewish court) and other priests would walk ahead of the officiating priest, creating a pathway of holiness toward the ceremonial site.

At the site of the ceremony, on the Mount of Olives facing the Temple, a ritual bath would be prepared in advance. This wasn't just any ritual bath - it had been specially constructed to ensure the highest standards of ritual purity. When the officiating priest arrived, he encountered a deeply moving moment. The elders would place their hands upon his head, investing him with their authority and blessing, and declare with gravity, "My master, the High Priest! Immerse yourself once!"

This form of address - calling him "High Priest" even though he might be a regular priest - emphasized the extraordinary importance of his role in this ceremony. After his immersion and careful drying, he would don the sacred priestly garments, preparing himself for the sacred task ahead.

The Journey of the Heifer

The transportation of the red heifer to the ceremony site required extraordinary measures. A special causeway was constructed specifically for this purpose, elevating the heifer's path above the ground. This remarkable architectural feature served a crucial purpose - to prevent any possibility of the heifer becoming ritually impure through contact with areas that might contain buried human remains.

This causeway, known in Hebrew as a "*gesher*" (bridge), represented a remarkable feat of ancient engineering. It extended from the Temple Mount across the Kidron Valley to the Mount of Olives, ensuring that the heifer's journey would maintain its perfect state of purity until the moment of the ceremony.

The Preparation of the Pyre

The construction of the wood pyre for burning the heifer was an art in itself. The priests would carefully select wood from specific types of trees - cedar, pine, cypress, or fig - each chosen for its particular qualities. The arrangement of this wood wasn't random but followed a precise architectural design, creating a tower that tapered as it rose, with carefully planned spaces for air circulation.

This precise arrangement served multiple purposes. The tapering design helped control the burn rate, while the air spaces ensured complete combustion. The choice of woods wasn't merely practical - each type carried symbolic significance in Jewish tradition. Cedar, for instance, represented strength and permanence, while the humble hyssop symbolized humility.

The Ceremony Itself

The actual ceremony combined solemn dignity with precise ritual actions. The heifer was positioned atop the wooden structure with extraordinary care - its head to the south and facing westward toward the Temple, bound with special cords made from reed grass. The choice of reed grass for the bindings wasn't arbitrary - like the stone chambers, reed grass was chosen because it wouldn't become a source of ritual impurity.

The priest would ascend the structure and position himself on the eastern side, facing west toward the Temple. The slaughter of the heifer required exceptional skill - the priest had to gather the blood in his left hand while maintaining his balance atop the wooden structure. The subsequent sprinkling of the blood seven times with his right index finger constituted a moment of intense concentration and precision.

After descending, the priest would ignite the pyre from its western side, maintaining the ceremony's geographical orientation toward the Temple. The addition of the cedar wood, hyssop, and scarlet-dyed wool — each tied together in a specific manner — had to be timed perfectly, cast into the flames at precisely the right moment.

The Creation and Distribution of the Ashes

Once the fire had completely consumed the heifer and the additional elements, and the ashes had cooled, the meticulous process of gathering and preparing the ashes began. Every particle was carefully collected and ground to a fine powder. This grinding process was considered so important that special tools were designated for this purpose alone.

Once prepared, the new ashes would be mixed with remnants of previous ones, creating a continuous chain that linked each preparation to all those that came before.

The distribution of the resulting ashes followed a carefully prescribed pattern, divided into three portions, each with its specific purpose:

- One portion was kept in the Temple itself, stored in a special chamber in the wall before the Women's Court, ready for immediate use when needed.

- A second portion was maintained at the site of the burning on the Mount of Olives, serving as a reserve supply.
- The third portion, kept in the Temple as a "remembrance," was never used but served as a permanent testament to the ceremony's eternal significance.

The Paradox of Purification

Perhaps the most profound aspect of the ceremony lies in its concluding moments. The priests involved in the preparation of these purifying ashes themselves became ritually impure. They had to wash both themselves and their garments in running water and remain in a state of ritual impurity until evening.

This ancient ceremony, with its intricate details and profound symbolism, represents far more than a series of ritual actions. It embodies the Jewish understanding that the physical and spiritual realms are deeply interconnected and that achieving the highest levels of spiritual purity requires extraordinary attention to physical detail and human intention.

CHAPTER FIVE

The Purification Ritual: Restoring Spiritual Purity

Understanding Ritual Impurity From Death

The laws of ritual impurity from death represent one of the most profound concepts in Jewish religious law. While the Book of Numbers, Chapter 19, provides detailed instructions for both contracting and purifying this severe form of spiritual impurity through the ashes of the red heifer, these ancient laws often challenge our modern understanding of spirituality and ritual practice.

At its core, ritual impurity is a spiritual state entirely distinct from physical uncleanliness. It applies exclusively to Jews - non-Jews neither contract nor transmit ritual impurity. When in this state, Jews are prohibited from touching or consuming consecrated objects and may not enter the Temple grounds. Additionally, priests and nazirites face specific restrictions, being forbidden from intentionally exposing themselves to death-related impurity.

What sets death-related impurity apart is both its severity and its unique transmission properties. While most forms of ritual impurity can be resolved through immersion in a ritual bath, death-related impurity demands a complex purification process involving the ashes of the red heifer. Moreover, this form of impurity is remarkably transmissible - one need not directly contact a dead body to become impure. Simply sharing an enclosed space with a dead body is sufficient for transmission.

This has particular relevance in our modern world. A person visiting a hospital, for instance, might unknowingly contract this impurity if there is a dead body anywhere in the building. Airplanes frequently transport the dead. Even riding in an elevator that previously carried a dead body could potentially transmit this impurity. Through such examples, we can appreciate how these ancient religious concepts continue to intersect with contemporary life, challenging us to consider their deeper spiritual significance in our modern world.

The Seven-Day Journey to Purity

The purification process for ritual impurity resulting from proximity to a dead body spans seven days, reflecting the spiritual significance of the number seven in Jewish tradition. This week-long journey mirrors other seven-day cycles in Jewish life, such as the days of creation and the seven days of mourning. The process is not merely about waiting a prescribed time but involves specific actions on particular days.

The crucial moments in this process occur on the third and seventh days when the impure person must be sprinkled with the special purification waters containing the ashes of the red heifer. This dual sprinkling represents a profound spiritual progression - the third day marking the initial separation from impurity, and the seventh day completing the transformation back to a state of ritual purity.

The Sacred Waters

The preparation of the purification waters involves several precise requirements that distinguish it from other ritual waters in Jewish law. While a standard ritual bath can use collected rainwater, the water for the red heifer ceremony must come from a natural spring - what the Bible calls "living water." This requirement emphasizes the life-giving nature of the purification process.

During the Temple period, this water was typically drawn from the Pool of Siloam in Jerusalem, a natural spring that still flows today. The choice of this particular source wasn't arbitrary - its location near the Temple Mount and its natural spring status made it ideal for this sacred purpose.

The Role of Children in Purity

One of the purification ritual's most fascinating aspects was the involvement of children specially raised for this purpose. Pregnant women, specifically wives of priests, were brought to live in specially prepared courtyards in Jerusalem. These courtyards contained houses built on solid bedrock to prevent the possibility of unknown graves beneath, ensuring the children would not become ritually impure. The children remained in these courtyards until they were eight years old, with everything they needed provided within the enclosed space, completely protected from any ritual impurity.

These children would gather the water used to prepare the "waters of sanctification" which would purify the priest assigned to burn the new heifer and prepare its ashes. Their involvement was a practical necessity to maintain the strictest level of purity.

When they came of age, pairs of oxen were prepared with boards set across their backs forming a platform. The children rode out of the courtyards atop these oxen, sitting on the boards. The boards created a bridge above any possible sources of impurity they might cross on the way to the Shiloach Spring. The children carried stone vessels to hold the water they gathered. Stone does not receive or impart ritual impurity.

The children would bring the spring water to the entrance of the women's court in the Temple where a stone vessel known as the *kelal,* which held the ashes of the red heifer, was kept at all times. One of the children took from these ashes and mixed the proper amount into the water, preparing the mixture of "waters of sanctification." Then, the children sprinkled the attending priest.

It has been suggested that including children in the ceremony represented the ideal of pure intention embodied in children. Their simple belief and pure service imbued the ceremony with a natural purity.

The Sprinkling Ceremony

The actual sprinkling ceremony combined sublime simplicity with precise detail. A tiny amount of the red heifer's ashes - even a particle as small as a mustard seed was sufficient - would be mixed with the spring water in a ritually pure vessel. Three stalks of hyssop, bound together according to specific requirements, were then used for the sprinkling.

The choice of hyssop carried deep significance. This humble plant, mentioned throughout the Bible in purification contexts, symbolizes humility and submission to divine will. King David referenced this symbolism in Psalm 51:9, pleading, "Purify me with hyssop, and I shall be clean."

The sprinkling itself required specific expertise. A ritually pure priest would dip the hyssop bundle into the mixture and sprinkle it toward the person requiring purification. Remarkably, even the smallest droplet of this water was sufficient to effect purification, demonstrating that spiritual transformation often depends more on quality than quantity.

The Paradox of Purification Continues

In a continuation of the paradox we saw in the preparation

of the ashes, everyone involved in the purification ritual - except for the priest who performed the sprinkling - would become ritually impure until evening and require immersion in a ritual bath. This recurring theme emphasizes the profound nature of the transformation being effected.

Beyond the Borders of Israel

During the Second Temple period, an additional dimension was added to these laws through a rabbinic decree issued by Jose ben Jo'ezer of Zeredah and Jose ben Johanan of Jerusalem. They declared that all lands outside of Israel would carry a certain degree of ritual impurity. This decree had far-reaching implications for Jewish life in the Diaspora. Anyone returning to Israel from abroad would be considered impure and require purification with the ashes of a red heifer.

The reasoning behind this decree reveals deep rabbinic concern for maintaining the purity of the priesthood. In lands outside Israel, graves were often unmarked or unknown, creating a constant risk for priests who might unknowingly become impure. The decree was particularly focused on protecting priests from eating their sacred portions in a state of impurity, which carried severe spiritual consequences.

This ancient decree continues to influence Jewish law today, contributing to the understanding that leaving the Land of Israel involves a certain degree of spiritual compromise. It underscores the unique spiritual status of the Holy Land and adds another layer to the modern significance of the red heifer ritual.

The Contemporary Implications

In our current reality, without the ashes of the red heifer, the state of ritual impurity from death remains unresolvable. This situation affects numerous aspects of Jewish life and particularly impacts the possibility of reinstating the full Temple service. While certain Temple offerings could theoretically be brought even in a state of impurity, many crucial aspects of Temple service require the complete ritual purity that only the red heifer's ashes can provide.

Understanding these laws helps us appreciate why the recent arrival of potential red heifers in Israel has generated such excitement and controversy. The restoration of this purification ritual would represent not just a historical revival but a fundamental transformation in the spiritual possibilities available to the Jewish people and, indeed, to all humanity.

The intricate details of the purification ritual remind us that spiritual transformation often requires precise physical actions that transcend understanding or intent. In the carefully choreographed dance between the physical and spiritual realms that characterizes Jewish ritual life, the red heifer's purification ceremony demonstrates how ancient rituals remain profoundly relevant to contemporary Jewish life, even as their full meaning lies beyond human comprehension.

CHAPTER SIX

The Test Run: Rediscovering Ancient Wisdom

W HEN PROFESSOR ZOHAR Amar first mentioned his plan to burn a cow in the Judean hills, his colleagues at Bar-Ilan University thought he had lost his mind. It was 2019, and the respected Land of Israel Studies professor had already made a name for himself identifying biblical plants and analyzing ancient dyes. But this was different. He wasn't just studying ancient texts or examining archaeological remains; he intended to recreate one of Judaism's most mysterious rituals: the burning of the red heifer.

"Everyone always talks about how one red heifer could purify the entire nation," Amar explained in his modest office, surrounded by books and botanical specimens. "But nobody had ever tested it. Nobody knew exactly how much ash one cow would produce, or how many people it could actually purify. These weren't just theoretical questions - they were practical ones that needed answers."

Amar's journey to this experiment began decades earlier. As a young researcher in the 1990s, he spent countless hours in the archives of the Cairo Genizah, the famous repository of ancient Jewish manuscripts. Among fragments of medieval texts, he found detailed descriptions of Temple-related measurements that sparked his curiosity. But one practice remained particularly enigmatic - the red heifer ceremony.

"I remember finding a fragment from the 12th century," Amar recalls, "where a rabbi described watching a cow being burned in a traditional Indian funeral pyre. He tried to understand the mechanics of the red heifer ceremony by comparing it to practices in other cultures. This told me that Jews throughout history had been trying to understand the practical aspects of this ritual."

The turning point came in 2018 when Amar received an unexpected call from a colleague in India. Dr. Rajesh Kumar, an expert in traditional cremation practices, had read Amar's papers on biblical ceremonies. "He told me something fascinating," Amar says. "The traditional funeral pyres in Varanasi achieve complete cremation, including bones, using specific wood arrangements that have been passed down for generations. It made me wonder - what if the ancient Temple priests used similar techniques?"

Armed with this insight, Amar began assembling his team. He recruited experts in archaeology, chemistry, and animal science. Dr. Sarah Cohen, a forensic anthropologist, joined to study the bone calcification process. David Levy, an ancient Middle Eastern architecture expert, helped design the burning site.

The preparation took months. Following ancient specifications, workers carved a trough into the bedrock that was 4.2 meters long, two meters wide, and 90 centimeters deep. "The dimensions weren't arbitrary," explains Levy. "We found that this size creates optimal air circulation for sustained high temperatures."

The wood arrangement proved crucial .This wasn't just a

bonfire but a carefully engineered structure described in the Talmud as a "tower with windows." Dr. Michael Berg, a chemical engineer who joined the team, explains: "The ancient design is remarkably sophisticated. The layered arrangement of different wood types creates a natural furnace effect."

They started with a foundation of pine needles and small twigs for initial ignition. Above this came dried fig trunks, chosen for their steady burning properties. The final layer consisted of oak logs, known for maintaining intense heat. "The spaces between the logs - the 'windows' mentioned in ancient texts - weren't decorative," Berg notes. "They created perfect airflow patterns for maximum combustion efficiency."

Finding the right cow took time. "We selected a mature sick heifer from the Baladi breed," Amar explains. "This was the type of cattle common in ancient Israel. While it wasn't red, its size and bone structure matched what we believe ancient red heifers would have been like."

The day of the burning arrived on a clear spring morning. Twelve men, following the ancient tradition, lifted the 270-kilogram cow onto the pyre using a specially prepared litter. They positioned it precisely - with its head on the south side, and its face westward. Its legs were on the west side, adhering to biblical specifications. Rabbi Yehuda Glick, a Temple Mount activist present that day, remembers the atmosphere: "Even though this was a scientific experiment, you could feel the weight of history. We were recreating something that hadn't been done for 2,000 years."

What happened next surprised even the skeptics. The intense heat caused the cow's belly to collapse within an hour - exactly as ancient sources had described. At this crucial moment, following biblical instructions, the team added cedar wood, hyssop, and scarlet-dyed wool to the fire. Their instruments recorded temperatures reaching 940 degrees Celsius.

"The heat was incredible," recalls Sarah Cohen. "Modern crematoriums operate at similar temperatures, but they're enclosed systems with gas burners. Achieving this in an open-air setting using just wood - it showed how sophisticated the ancient technique was."

The burning continued for nine hours. Graduate students worked in shifts, recording temperature readings and documenting the progressive breakdown of different tissues. "We observed complete calcination of the bones," Cohen reports. "Even the densest parts of the skeleton were reduced to ash, just as the ancient texts described."

After several days of cooling, the team began the meticulous process of collecting and analyzing the ashes. The numbers were astounding. The experiment used 1.4 tons of wood and produced 66 kilograms of ash, with approximately 11 kilograms coming from the animal itself.

But the real revelation came when Amar calculated how many purification ceremonies this ash could theoretically perform. "Traditional sources say only a tiny amount of ash was needed for each ceremony," he explains. "We found that 0.2-0.3 grams of ash were sufficient for 250 liters of water. One sprinkling used just one-tenth of one milliliter of this mixture."

The mathematical conclusion was staggering: the ashes from this single burning could theoretically provide 660 billion individual purification ceremonies. Adding another ton of wood to the burning would enable another 250 billion sprinklings.

News of these findings spread rapidly. Agricultural scientists from Nebraska to New Zealand contacted Amar about his wood-to-flesh burning ratios. Archaeologists studying ancient purification rituals in other cultures found striking parallels. A delegation of Hindu priests from Varanasi visited the site, confirming similarities with their traditional practices.

The implications extended beyond religious circles.

Environmental scientists noted the efficiency of the ancient burning technique. Forensic experts found the ash-collection methods relevant to their work. A team from MIT expressed interest in the wood arrangement's unique properties.

The significance of Amar's work became even clearer in 2022 when five potential red heifers arrived in Israel. His experimental protocols suddenly provided crucial practical guidance. Temple Institute representatives consulted his findings about wood requirements, temperature levels, and ash yields.

"Science hasn't displaced the mystery," Amar reflects in his office, surrounded by data printouts and ancient texts. "If anything, it's deepened it. We showed that our ancestors knew exactly what they were doing. One red heifer really could purify millions upon millions of people. The mathematics are extraordinary."

As Israel prepares for the possibility of performing this ceremony for the first time in two millennia, Amar's research provides both practical guidance and spiritual inspiration. It reminds us that ancient wisdom often contains depths we're only beginning to fathom. Sometimes it takes modern science to help us fully appreciate just how sophisticated our ancestors really were.

CHAPTER SEVEN

Messianic Implications: The Tenth Red Heifer

THROUGHOUT HISTORY, CERTAIN moments stand out as turning points—events that mark the boundary between one era and another. In Jewish tradition, the appearance of a perfect red heifer has always been such a moment. Since God first commanded this mysterious ritual at Mount Sinai, only nine red heifers have been used in Temple service. Each marked a pivotal chapter in Jewish history, and, according to ancient prophecy, the tenth is destined to herald the messianic age.

The Nine Red Heifers: A Journey Through History

The story of these nine red heifers mirrors the journey of the Jewish people themselves. The first, prepared by Moses himself in the wilderness, came at a crucial moment. Moses performed the ceremony shortly after completing the Tabernacle—on the second day of the Hebrew month of Nisan, one year after the Exodus. This timing was significant, as it allowed the entire nation to purify themselves before the approaching Passover festival. According to the Sages, this first red heifer atoned specifically for the sin of the Golden Calf - a red cow purifying the sin of worshipping a golden one.

The second red heifer emerged during one of the most dramatic periods of Jewish return. When Ezra led the Jews back from Babylonian exile in 457 BCE, they found Jerusalem in ruins. The returning exiles needed purification before they could begin rebuilding the Temple. As recorded in ancient texts, this second red heifer was miraculously provided—appearing in precisely the right place and time.

Seven more red heifers were prepared during the Second Temple period. Each has its own remarkable story. The third was prepared under the supervision of Simon the Just, whose righteousness was so great that the Western light of the Temple Menorah never went out during his forty years as High Priest. The fourth came during the time of Johanan the High Priest, who later became a Sadducee, adding a layer of controversy to its preparation.

The fifth red heifer coincided with the rise of the Pharisaic movement, while the sixth emerged during the time of the great debates between the Houses of Hillel and Shammai. The seventh and eighth appeared during times of relative peace, allowing for the continued operation of the Temple service. Rabbi Judah HaNasi records that the ninth red heifer, prepared by the High Priest Ishmael Ben Piavi around 60 CE, was used to maintain ritual purity for three centuries after the Temple's destruction. Some sources suggest that priests managed to preserve small amounts of these ashes, hiding them for safekeeping and future use. The Talmud hints at locations where these ashes might have been concealed, though their whereabouts remain one of history's great mysteries.

Attempts Through the Ages

Despite the destruction of the Second Temple, the search for red heifers never ceased. The hope of finding another suitable candidate persisted, inspiring generations to continue the quest across centuries and continents. Medieval records recount numerous efforts, including letters sent to Maimonides in 1165 about a potential red heifer in Egypt—though he ultimately deemed it unsuitable. Similarly, the renowned traveler Benjamin of Tudela documented rumors of red heifers in remote Jewish communities in Arabia.

During the 16th century, Rabbi Moshe Alshich wrote of an intensive search throughout the Ottoman Empire. In 1889, a group of rabbis in Poland thought they had found a candidate, leading to extensive correspondence with Jerusalem's rabbinical authorities. The early Zionist period saw renewed efforts, with agricultural settlements specifically breeding cattle with this goal in mind.

The Prophetic Dimension

The efforts to find a suitable red heifer were not merely about fulfilling ritual requirements; they were driven by the belief that the red heifer would play a central role in the ultimate redemption, as foretold in prophetic texts. Ezekiel envisions divine purification, declaring "I will sprinkle pure water upon you, and you shall be purified: I will purify you from all your defilement and from all your fetishes" (Ezekiel 36:25). Similarly, Isaiah's promise that "though your sins be as scarlet, they shall be white as snow," understood by some as an allusion to the transformative power of the red heifer's ashes.

This prophetic association gained further emphasis in later Jewish thought. In the 10th century, Rabbi Saadia Gaon listed the red heifer among the ten signs that would precede the messianic era. The Zohar, Judaism's primary mystical text, contains cryptic references to the "red cow that will awaken from the north" in the end of days.

Debates Over Timing and Sequence

While the prophetic texts outline the red heifer's pivotal role in the messianic era, scholars and sages have long debated its precise timing and sequence within the unfolding of redemption. Does its appearance precede the Messiah, or does the Messiah bring it with him? The question has profound implications for how we interpret current events.

Maimonides seems clear in his position that the Messiah himself will prepare the tenth red heifer. However, Rabbi Chaim Kanievsky, who was one of the leading Torah authorities of our generation until his passing in 2022, suggested a different view. "The red heifer could come before the Messiah," he wrote, "as part of the preparation for his arrival, just as Elijah the Prophet will come first to prepare the way."

Rabbi Menachem Mendel Schneerson, the late rabbi of the Lubavitch Hasidic dynasty, spoke often about the red heifer's connection to redemption. He pointed out that, unlike other Temple-related commandments, the red heifer was performed outside the Temple grounds. "This teaches us," he explained, "that sometimes preparation for holiness must begin in the seemingly ordinary realm, outside the obvious boundaries of sanctity."

The rabbi's statement suggests that preparations for restoring Temple worship can begin with peripheral elements like the red heifer ritual. While preparing the ashes would bring us one step closer to the Third Temple's eventual restoration, it would not require immediate changes to the Temple Mount. The full significance of this preparatory step would only become apparent once Temple service is restored.

Modern Developments and Preparations

The current search for the red heifer involves unprecedented cooperation between various Jewish communities. The Temple

Institute in Jerusalem has established detailed protocols for examining potential candidates, combining traditional requirements with modern genetic testing.

The involvement of Christian ranchers in raising potential red heifers has sparked fascinating theological discussions. Some see it as the fulfillment of Isaiah's prophecy that "the sons of strangers shall build up thy walls" (Isaiah 60:10). Others point to the biblical precedent of King Cyrus, a non-Jewish monarch who assisted in rebuilding the Temple.

Global Jewish Perspectives

The possibility of a tenth red heifer has sparked different reactions across the Jewish world. Sephardic Chief Rabbi Yitzchak Yosef has called for careful validation of any potential candidate, emphasizing the gravity of such a finding. "We must be absolutely certain," he stated, "as this impacts the entire Jewish people."

In Hasidic communities, the news has been received with a mixture of excitement and careful restraint. The rabbi of the Hasidic dynasty of Belz taught that discussing the red heifer's return helps bring it closer to reality. Meanwhile, traditional Jewish religious academies of the Lithuanian tradition have increased their study of the laws regarding the red heifer, viewing this as practical preparation for what might come.

Practical Preparations

The Temple Institute has moved beyond theoretical preparation. They've created specialized vessels for the ceremony, trained priests in the precise details of the ritual, and even designated specific areas on the Mount of Olives for the potential ceremony.

Rabbi Azariah Ariel, an expert in Temple rituals, describes the extensive preparations: "We've reconstructed every aspect of the ceremony based on ancient sources. The priests practice the movements, the sprinkling patterns, everything. When the time comes, we'll be ready."

The Broader Implications

The return of the red heifer ceremony would impact far more than just Temple service. According to Jewish law, everyone today carries ritual impurity from the dead, affecting our relationship with sacred space and objects. The red heifer's purifying power would enable a new level of spiritual connection.

The ceremony's philosophical impact is equally profound, as Rabbi David Lau, Israel's former Ashkenazi Chief Rabbi, notes: "The red heifer represents the ultimate paradox - it purifies the impure while making the pure impure. This teaches us that sometimes spiritual growth requires embracing apparent contradictions."

Signs of the Times

Many have pointed to developments surrounding the red heifer as one of many signs that suggest the messianic era is approaching. The convergence of so many factors - the return of Jews to Israel, the recovery of ancient Temple knowledge, and now the appearance of potential red heifers - strikes many as more than coincidence. Rabbi Shlomo Amar, former Sephardic Chief Rabbi, sees it as part of a larger pattern: "We are witnessing the gradual unfoldment of redemption, each development building upon the previous ones."

Rabbi Chaim Richman, the International Director of the Temple Institute, similarly commented on the institute's website: "If there has been no red heifer for the past 2,000 years, perhaps it is because the time was not right; Israel was far from being ready. But now... what could it mean for the times we live in, to have the means for purification so close at hand? With the words of Maimonides in mind, we cannot help but wonder and pray: If there are now red heifers... is ours the era that will need them?" In addition, the heifers were brought to Israel just before the Hebrew year 5783, represented by the Hebrew letter תשפג, began. Some suggest that these letters are an acronym for "It will be a year of the red heifer of redemption" (תהיה שנת פרת גאולה). The previous two years formed similar acronyms, creating a three-year sequence that many find remarkable. While not definitive signs, such patterns could add another layer of meaning to current events.

Looking Forward

As we reflect on the historical journey, the prophetic significance, and the modern preparations, the red heifer emerges as both a symbol of continuity and a beacon of hope for the future. Standing at what might be the threshold of a new era, the red heifer embodies both challenge and promise. It challenges us to prepare for redemption while remaining grounded in practical realities, promises that purification is achievable, and reminds us that spiritual renewal can emerge from the most unlikely sources.

Rabbi Binny Freedman, Educational Director of the Isralight Institute, saw profound relevance in the red heifer ritual for modern times:

"We live in a world divided between those who glorify death and those who choose life," Rabbi Freedman said. "The red heifer, which transforms death's impurity into life's renewal, speaks directly to this struggle."

His words take on an added dimension when considering that Rabbi Freedman was inside Jerusalem's Sbarro restaurant in August 2001, when a Palestinian terrorist set off an explosive vest, murdering 15 Israelis and wounding many others.

Whether we stand on the cusp of the messianic era or still

have a long journey ahead, the red heifer reminds us that redemption often comes through paradox, that unity can emerge from division, and that ancient wisdom continues to illuminate our path forward. As we witness developments that our ancestors could only dream of, we're reminded that sometimes the most profound changes begin with something as simple as a perfectly red cow.

(photo credit, Boneh Israel)

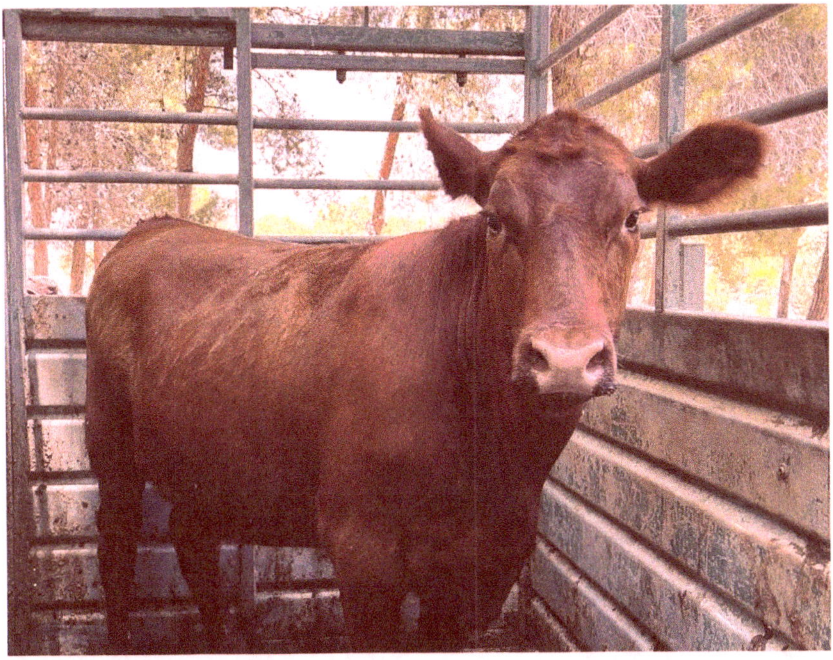

(photo credit, Boneh Israel)

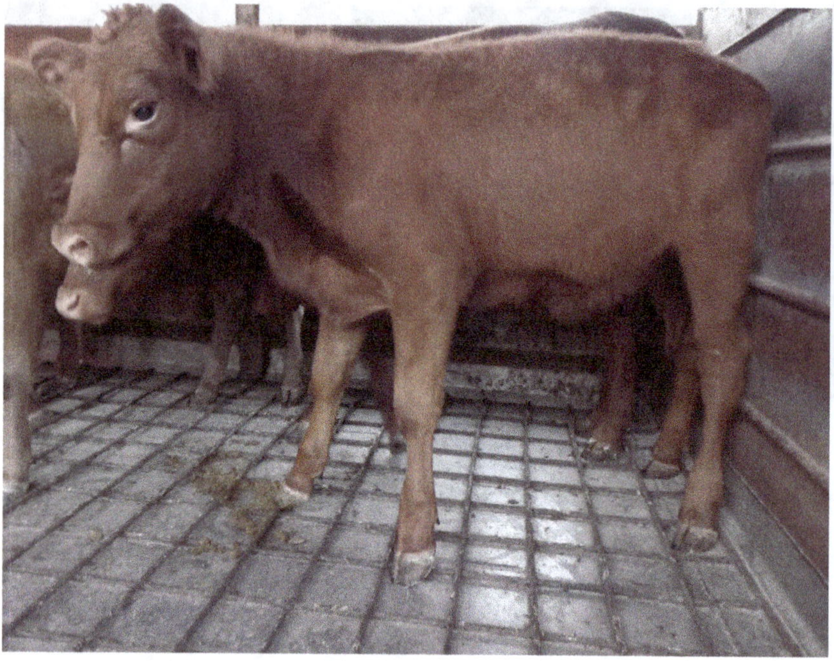

(photo credit, Boneh Israel)

(photo credit, Larry Borntrager)

Larry Borntrager, a volunteer from Indiana, takes care of the red heifers in Shiloh

Israel365 Young Leadership Tour visits the red heifers in Shiloh (courtesy, Israel365)

(photo credit, Larry Borntrager)

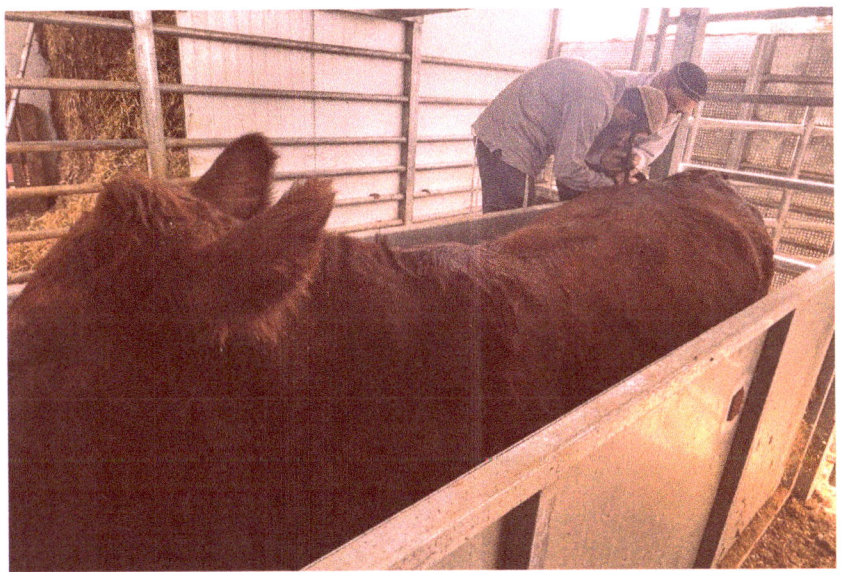

Rabbis inspecting the red heifers for non-red hairs (photo credit, Larry Borntrager)

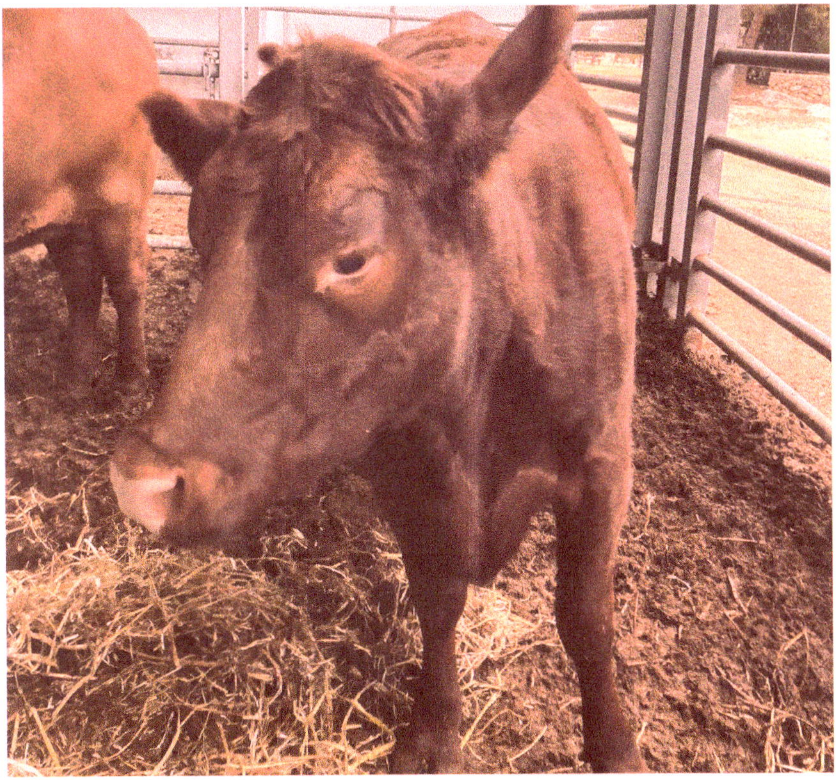

(photo credit, Larry Borntrager)

CHAPTER EIGHT

The Red Heifer Program: A Modern Search For Ancient Purity

I N THE HEART of Jerusalem's Old City, behind the heavy wooden doors of the Temple Institute's research center, a remarkable scene unfolds daily. Rabbis huddle over high-resolution photographs of red cows sent from around the world. Scientists discuss genetic markers with cattle breeders. Priests practice the intricate movements of purification ceremonies that haven't been performed for two millennia. This is the headquarters of the most organized attempt in history to restore one of Judaism's most mysterious commandments - the ritual of the red heifer.

The Institute's Systematic Approach

The Temple Institute's "Raise a Red Heifer" program, launched in 2015, represents a convergence of ancient wisdom and modern technology. Founded in 1987, the Institute has already recreated over 60 sacred vessels for use in the Third Temple. From the golden candelabrum to the High Priest's breastplate, these vessels can be viewed at their visitors center in Jerusalem's Old

City. But the red heifer presents unique challenges that require an unprecedented level of precision and patience.

"For us to perform this *mitzvah* (commandment), we need a kosher red heifer to be born," explains Rabbi Azariah Ariel, who heads the Institute's red heifer program. "This is in the hands of God. We know that this is rare, but we don't even have the statistics to guess how rare this actually is in nature. Even the ranchers we interviewed have no idea."

The Institute maintains a sophisticated protocol for evaluating potential candidates. Every reported red calf undergoes an initial photographic screening. If promising, experts conduct in-person examinations using specialized equipment to analyze hair color at the microscopic level. The Institute has developed a custom color chart defining exactly what shade of red qualifies as "red" according to Jewish law.

Unexpected Discoveries

While the Institute pursues its systematic approach in Jerusalem, remarkable stories of red heifer sightings continue to emerge from unexpected corners of the world. In the sun-drenched hills of Baja, Mexico, Rabbi Benny "Bentsion" Hershcovich's discovery of what appeared to be a red heifer during a routine kosher milk inspection captured worldwide attention.

"I've grown up with the stories, so I know how rare and valuable the red heifer is," Rabbi Hershcovich recalls. "I've never seen a red heifer and I never expected to see one. My heart literally jumped when I saw it." The local farmer's puzzlement at the rabbi's excitement only added to the story's charm - here was a potentially sacred cow, peacefully grazing among ordinary cattle, its owner entirely unaware of its significance.

Similar tales have emerged across the globe. In West Virginia, retired civil engineer Bill Shuff found a promising candidate among his son's cattle. In New Jersey, Herbert Celler's red heifer drew thousands of visitors and even attracted a million-dollar offer, which he declined on principle. "Some things," Celler said, "are beyond money."

The Genetic Frontier: Modern Questions, Ancient Answers

Renewing the red heifer ceremony requires delving into intricate rituals that have not been seen for two millennia. Every one of the myriad details must be addressed.

In many cases, modern physical reality has changed from ancient times, requiring Jewish religious law to be adapted accordingly. The rabbinic scholars at the Temple Institute don't make these adaptations based on personal opinion. Instead, they carefully examine traditional Jewish texts and commentaries, searching for even the smallest relevant details. These scholars follow a strict, systematic process of interpreting religious law, a method in which they have received extensive training. When it comes to determining these religious requirements, there can be no uncertainty or compromise, as fulfilling these divine commandments is considered of utmost importance.

The Institute's most ambitious initiative involves modern genetic science. Working with leading Israeli agricultural laboratories, they've begun mapping the genes responsible for cattle coloration. Dr. Sarah Goldman, a geneticist collaborating with the project, explains: "We're identifying specific genetic markers that produce the exact shade of red required by Jewish law. It's fascinating how ancient religious texts can guide modern scientific research."

The program faced initial skepticism from both religious and scientific communities. Some rabbis questioned whether genetically engineered cattle would fulfill the biblical requirements, and scientists wondered about dedicating research resources to such an esoteric goal. But as Dr. Goldman notes, "The project has yielded valuable insights into bovine genetics that have applications far beyond our specific purpose."

Training the Priests

Another aspect of preparation takes place in a quiet courtyard on Jerusalem's outskirts. Here, descendants of the biblical priests practice the intricate ceremonies associated with the red heifer ritual. Using specially crafted vessels and precise measurements of water and ash, they rehearse movements that haven't been performed in two millennia.

"We can't wait until we find the perfect heifer to start training," explains Rabbi Yehoshua Cohen, who oversees the preparation program. "Every aspect must be perfect - the angle of sprinkling, the direction of movement, even the priest's intention during the ceremony."

The training involves modern technology. High-speed cameras analyze the spray patterns of the sprinkling ceremony, and computer models simulate the optimal construction of the burning site. Yet the essence remains deeply traditional, passed down through generations of priests who maintained this knowledge even when its practical application seemed impossible.

Global Collaboration

The search for the red heifer has created unexpected alliances. Christian ranchers in Texas have offered their expertise and facilities. Hindu scholars from India have shared insights about their ancient cattle-breeding practices. Muslim archaeologists have provided valuable information about historical cattle-raising in the Middle East.

Social media has revolutionized the search, enabling instant global communication and collaboration. The Institute maintains WhatsApp groups with international ranchers who alert them to potential candidates. Their Facebook page receives daily photographs of red calves from every continent. "Twenty years ago, finding a red heifer meant traveling for weeks," Rabbi Ariel notes. "Now we can make initial assessments instantly from Jerusalem."

The Economics of Hope

The program's financial aspects reflect its complexity. The Institute's annual budget for red heifer research exceeds $1 million, funded entirely by donations. Beyond direct research costs, they maintain relationships with ranchers globally, fund genetic research, and support the priest training program.

Yet the economic impact extends further. When word spreads of a potential red heifer, local communities often experience mini-tourism booms. Herbert Celler's New Jersey farm drew over 37,000 visitors before his heifer was disqualified. In addition, a small industry has emerged around the search, from specialized cattle brokers to manufacturers of examination equipment.

Preparing the Ground

An area on Jerusalem's Mount of Olives has already been designated for the future ceremony. Archaeological surveys confirm it corresponds to the location used during Temple times. The Institute has prepared detailed architectural plans for the burning site, incorporating ancient requirements with modern safety standards.

The latest development involves establishing a specialized quarantine facility near Jerusalem to ensure the heifer remains ritually pure until it reaches the required age. "When we find a suitable heifer," Rabbi Ariel explains, "we'll need to transport it to Israel and maintain its perfect status until it reaches the required age. This facility ensures we can control every aspect of its environment."

Looking Forward

As technology advances and understanding deepens, the Temple Institute's work continues with renewed vigor. "We're not just searching for a cow," Rabbi Richman reflects. "We're preparing for a renewed connection to ancient wisdom, a bridge between past and future."

The quest for the red heifer embodies a uniquely Jewish approach: combining meticulous practical preparation with unwavering faith. Whether through genetic science, global networking, or traditional breeding, the search continues. And perhaps, as these scholars suggest, the very act of searching helps prepare the world for what they believe will ultimately come.

"Our goal in the heifer program, and everything we do at the institute, is to create the longing for the Temple in the heart of the Jewish people," Rabbi Richman concludes. "How it comes about? That has yet to be seen. But when it does, we'll be ready."

As these efforts converge, the search for the red heifer stands as a testament to the enduring interplay of ancient tradition and modern innovation—an act of faith, hope, and preparation for a future that remains shrouded in mystery yet steeped in promise. In the meantime, the work continues: photographs are examined, genetic tests are conducted, priests practice their ceremonies, and somewhere—perhaps in a remote pasture or sophisticated breeding facility—the next potential red heifer may already be growing toward maturity, waiting to be discovered.

CHAPTER NINE

The Search: A Modern Exodus

O N A SCORCHING August afternoon in 2022, Byron Stinson sat in Tel Aviv's Ben Gurion Airport, his eyes glued to a flight tracker app on his phone. Five red heifers were making their way to Israel somewhere over the Atlantic Ocean, and Stinson wouldn't breathe easily until he saw their plane appear on his screen. After months of effort, countless setbacks, and seemingly endless bureaucratic hurdles, the dream of bringing red heifers to Israel was finally becoming reality - if they could just get the timing right.

The journey began years earlier when the Temple Institute launched its red heifer program. Rabbi Azariah Ariel, tasked with finding suitable candidates and addressing complex Jewish legal issues, knew from the start that this would be no ordinary undertaking. Even in Temple times, when the ritual was actively practiced, finding a perfect red heifer was exceedingly rare.

But Ariel remained determined. "From our side, the ritual requirement was established at Mount Sinai," Rabbi Ariel said. '*Mitzvot* (commandments) are not optional; we do not wait for them to float down from heaven. As Jews, we must do what we can to perform what God commanded."

The Temple Institute's initial efforts focused on Israeli cattle ranchers. When this proved unsuccessful, they attempted to import fertilized red Angus embryos from the United States. Despite careful planning and significant investment, none of these embryos developed into appropriate candidates. The search seemed at an impasse—until an unexpected partnership emerged.

Enter Boneh Israel, a unique collaboration between Christians and Jews united in their desire to fulfill biblical prophecy. In 2022, while the Temple Institute was investigating the possibility of using genetic manipulation to produce a red heifer, Boneh Israel joined the search with a different approach - they would look for naturally born red calves on American cattle ranches.

The organization placed advertisements in cattle industry magazines, asking to be contacted if any unusually red calves were born. The response revealed both the challenges and the unexpected connections that would shape their mission. One rancher initially reported a red calf, only to later withdraw after his pastor warned him against helping to bring about the Third Temple. But such reactions were rare, as Byron Stinson, Boneh Israel's team leader, discovered.

"The Bible says to bring a red cow to purify Israel," Stinson explained, embodying the straightforward faith that drove the project. "I may not understand it, but I am just doing what the Bible said."

The breakthrough came when a cattle farmer in Comanche, Texas, about two and a half hours from Dallas, contacted them about five red calves born on his ranch.

What made these calves particularly special was an unexpected consequence of the COVID-19 pandemic. Typically, calves are ear-tagged when just a few days old - a procedure that would render them unfit for the Temple service. But when these calves were born, the ranch worker responsible for tagging was in quarantine, leaving the calves unmarked and potentially suitable for the commandment.

Finding the calves was just the beginning. The logistics of transporting live cattle from Texas to Israel proved to be a masterclass in problem-solving. Shipping by sea was ruled out as too stressful for the animals. Air transport seemed the obvious solution, but this introduced its own set of challenges.

The timing requirements were particularly daunting. Israeli law prohibits importing cattle older than one year, but the calves needed to be at least five months old to be weaned. This created a narrow window of time in which to transport the young animals. Adding to the complexity, airlines only fly livestock out of Texas in October due to summer heat - but by October, the cows would be too old for Israeli regulations.

The physical requirements were equally demanding. Any bruises or cuts could disqualify the heifers, requiring exceptionally gentle handling. Even identification posed a challenge - how do you permanently identify an animal that can't bear any marks or carry any burden?

Rabbi Ariel and his team tackled each challenge methodically. When considering identification methods, they first examined stomach boluses - devices that are permanently placed in the cow's stomach for identification. However, this was ruled out on religious grounds; the rabbis determined that carrying such a device would constitute bearing a burden, forbidden for a red heifer. After careful study, they found a solution: a subcutaneous RFID chip that could be inserted without leaving a scar.

The temperature requirements nearly derailed the entire project. In mid-August, when American Airlines finally agreed to fly the heifers to New York, a last-minute complication arose. While the temperature in New York was an acceptable 75 degrees Fahrenheit, Tel Aviv was forecast to be 86 degrees at the scheduled landing time - one degree above the maximum allowed.

"We knew the cows had been raised in Texas and were used to the heat," Stinson recalled, "but those were the regulations – so I flew back to Israel empty-handed."

With time running out, Boneh Israel made a bold decision. They arranged a 33-hour truck journey to transport the heifers to New York, where they spent three weeks in a horse pasture owned by Alex Nichols, a specialist in shipping horses. Working with Frank De Leede, who handles horse shipments from Israel, they began planning the final leg of the journey.

"The final arrangements were made in the last week before the flight to Israel, and we knew that if they didn't work, the deadline might pass and they would be too old," De Leede said. "I was sitting in Israel, my eyes glued to a flight tracker. Until I saw on the flight tracker that the plane was in the air, I wasn't sure Israel would have a red heifer."

The story of the red heifers' journey to Israel reflects a remarkable convergence of ancient prophecy and modern logistics. It required cooperation between Jews and Christians, expertise from cattle ranchers and shipping specialists, and solutions to problems ranging from subcutaneous chips to international temperature regulations.

For those involved, the project represented more than just transporting cattle. "The prophecies came true, and the Jews are back in Israel," Byron reflected. "Now they need to build a Temple. But it's like buying a really nice car. If you don't have the key, you aren't going anywhere. The red heifer is the key to making the Temple work like it should."

Rabbi Chaim Richman, the former International Director of the Temple Institute, also sees deep significance in the preparations being made for the renewal of the red heifer ritual: "It's not enough to just mourn the Temple. We have to move from mourning to building. The Jewish Temples are not myths; they stood here for 800 years as a place of purity in how we relate to each other and peace between nations. This human condition is sorely lacking and will return when a Temple stands again in Jerusalem."

The successful arrival of the red heifers in Israel marked not just the end of a complex logistical operation, but potentially the beginning of a new chapter in religious history.

While the arrival of these five red heifers represents an extraordinary milestone, the journey from candidate to qualification remains fraught with uncertainty.

On March 4, 2025, Rabbi Azariah Ariel, the head of the Temple Institute's Red Heifer Project, gave a Hebrew language interview, answering many of the questions concerning the project's recent developments. At the forefront was the suitability of the five red heifers brought to Israel by Boneh Israel. The heifers had long since passed the minimum age of two years, yet no preparations were being made to perform the ritual, causing concern.

"At this moment, it is unclear whether we have in our possession in Israel a red heifer that is verifiably kosher and suited for the ceremony. About two years ago, five excellent red calves were brought to Israel. They had been checked and certified in America as perfectly red but several months after they arrived, they began to grow white hairs. There is an ongoing discussion in the Temple Institute regarding their suitability and whether the proximity of the hairs to each other disqualifies the cows or not."

While the Bible clearly states that the heifers must be entirely red and the sages teach that there may not be two non-red hairs, these hairs may fall out, rendering the cow suited for the ceremony. For this reason, the red heifers in Shilo continue to be protected and occasionally inspected. They may also be the basis of a future project focused on breeding a perfectly red heifer.

The Jewish people have waited patiently for two millennia for the appearance of a truly kosher red heifer, and the standards cannot be compromised. Yet the remarkable progress made through this international effort has created unprecedented knowledge and infrastructure. When the time comes—whether with one of these heifers or another yet to be born—the groundwork has been laid, the expertise cultivated, and the spiritual readiness established for this pivotal step toward Temple restoration.

As the Temple Institute continues its preparation work, the arrival of these heifers represents more than just the potential fulfillment of a biblical commandment – it symbolizes the bridge between ancient wisdom and modern capability, between faith and action. Whether or not these particular heifers prove suitable for the Temple service, their journey shows how seemingly insurmountable challenges can be overcome through persistence, creativity, and collaboration between people of different faiths united by a common purpose.

CHAPTER TEN

Red Heifer from the Nations

T HE RECENT ACQUISITION of five red heifers through Boneh Israel has sparked profound discussions in religious circles, raising
intriguing questions about the role of non-Jews in Temple-related
matters. This contemporary development not only echoes ancient
debates but also highlights the delicate balance between safeguard-
ing the sanctity of Jewish ritual and acknowledging the potential of
Divine Providence to operate through unexpected means.

Historical Precedent in Jewish Law

The question of whether non-Jews may participate in providing elements for Temple service presents a complex tapestry
of Jewish legal considerations. While certain aspects of Temple
service are exclusively restricted to Jewish participation—such
as the half-shekel contribution and the daily offerings—the case
of the red heifer presents unique considerations that have been
debated by our Sages throughout history.

The primary source for this discussion appears in the Oral
Law (Mishna Para 2:1), where we find a fundamental debate
between Rabbi Eliezer and the other sages. Rabbi Eliezer took a

stringent position, arguing against purchasing a red heifer from gentiles due to concerns about potential invalidation through gentile handling. However, the majority opinion disagreed with this view, maintaining that such purchases were permissible. This more lenient position was later codified by Maimonides in his code of Jewish law (Hilchot Para Aduma 1:1), lending significant weight to the permissive approach.

The Remarkable Tale of Dama ben Netina

Perhaps the most compelling historical precedent for purchasing a red heifer for ritual use comes from the story of Dama ben Netina, a gentile merchant from Ashkelon during the Second Temple period (first century CE). This account, preserved in both the Babylonian and Jerusalem Talmuds, clearly demonstrates that the Temple authorities were willing to conduct business with non-Jewish merchants to obtain red heifers, providing practical historical evidence that such transactions were considered valid and acceptable.

In the Talmudic account, the Sages sought to purchase a precious stone from Dama to replace one that had fallen from the High Priest's breastplate. They offered him one hundred dinars, a considerable sum at the time. However, when Dama discovered that retrieving the gem would require disturbing his sleeping father, as the key to the lockbox lay beneath his father's pillow, he refused to complete the transaction.

Misinterpreting his refusal as a negotiation tactic, the Sages increased their offer to one thousand dinars. Yet Dama remained steadfast in his refusal to disturb his father's rest. Only when his father naturally awoke did Dama retrieve the gem. When the Sages attempted to pay him the higher amount they had offered, Dama nobly refused, accepting only the original price of one hundred dinars, declaring that he would not profit from the merit of honoring his father.

The Talmud relates that Heaven rewarded this extraordinary display of filial piety in a remarkable way—that very night, a perfect red heifer was born in Dama's herd. The Jews subsequently purchased this extremely rare animal from him for an enormous sum, far exceeding what he had foregone in the gem transaction. This account explicitly demonstrates a case where a red heifer was not only purchased from a non-Jew but where such a purchase was viewed as divinely orchestrated.

Additional Historical Evidence

This remarkable account, alongside others from Jewish tradition, further illustrates how righteous gentiles have played pivotal roles in enabling sacred practices. Further support for gentile participation comes from a fascinating homiletic statement by the Sages, found in *Sifre Zuta* (Bamidbar 19:2). This text records a discussion in which the companions of Rabbi Eliezer cited a practical precedent to counter his restrictive position. They referenced a case where a red heifer was successfully purchased from Arab merchants. While the text doesn't record Rabbi Eliezer's response to this evidence, the very existence of such a precedent strengthens the case for allowing non-Jewish participation in providing red heifers for Temple service.

Contemporary Implications

These historical sources and precedents have a significant bearing on modern efforts to reinstate the red heifer ritual. The fact that Boneh Israel's red heifers came through Christian-Jewish cooperation aligns with historical precedents like the story of Dama ben Netina, which teaches that Divine Providence sometimes works through unexpected channels, and that merit can come through those who show exceptional moral character, regardless of their religious affiliation. Just as the Sages of old recognized the legitimacy of obtaining a red heifer from righteous gentiles, today's religious authorities can draw upon these precedents when evaluating modern collaborative efforts to restore this crucial element of Temple service.

Universal Aspects of Temple Service

These historical examples not only provide practical precedent but also hint at the universal aspects of the Temple. While the Temple represents the unique relationship between God and the Jewish people, certain aspects of its function involve the broader human family, underscoring its role as a "house of prayer for all nations" (Isaiah 56:7).

This is expressed in the Temple service on the Feast of Tabernacles, when the nations come to the Temple. The Sages note that the number of bulls offered in the Temple during the holiday added up to 70, equal to the number of gentile nations listed in the Bible as the descendants of Noah, further hinting at the universal aspect of the Temple in Jerusalem.

This understanding aligns perfectly with our prophetic tradition, which envisions the Third Temple as a place where all of humanity will come to serve God, each according to their appropriate role and status. In this universal Temple, all of Israel will serve as priests for the nations (Exodus 19:6). The participation of righteous Gentiles in facilitating Temple-related matters, such as providing the red heifer, can be seen as a stepping stone toward this ultimate vision of universal divine service.

In this light, the current collaboration between Jews and Christians in reviving the commandment of the red heifer takes on additional significance. While maintaining clear boundaries and the unique role of the Jewish people in performing the actual Temple service, this cooperation may serve as a model for how different faith communities can work together toward shared spiritual goals while respecting their distinct roles and obligations. This collaboration not only mirrors historical precedents but also lays a foundation for future interfaith efforts. By respecting each tradition's unique role while working toward shared spiritual objectives, such initiatives point to a vision of unity that transcends divisions, reflecting the ultimate purpose of the Temple as a symbol of peace and divine connection for all humanity.

CHAPTER ELEVEN

Finding the Pure Priest: The Search for a Qualified Priest

The Temple Institute's Breakthrough

In the spring of 2024, the Temple Institute in Jerusalem made a remarkable announcement that captured the attention of those following preparations for the Third Temple. They had found a young priest who met the stringent requirements to perform the red heifer ceremony. This development marked another crucial step toward the potential restoration of Temple services, following the earlier milestone of finding suitable red heifers.

Origins of the Priesthood

The role of the priest traces back to biblical worship's very foundations. When God established the priesthood, He chose Aaron, Moses's brother, and his sons to serve as the priests for all future generations, as recorded in Exodus 28:1. As the descendants of Aaron, the priests are a subset of the tribe of Levi. As members of a tribe of Israel, Levites should have inherited a portion of the Land of Israel. However, to free them from work and allow them to focus on the Temple service and teaching the people, the Levites were dispersed among the other tribes and given a portion of the tithes instead. This divine selection created a hereditary priesthood that has maintained its distinct identity through more than three millennia of Jewish history, surviving exile, persecution, and dispersal across the globe.

Maintaining Priestly Identity Through Exile

Preserving the priestly lineage through history represents an extraordinary feat of cultural memory and dedication. During the First Temple period, the priests served in clearly defined shifts, with detailed records kept of their genealogy and service. When the Babylonians destroyed the First Temple in 586 BCE, these priestly families maintained their distinct identity even in exile. The prophet Ezekiel, himself a priest, continued to instruct the priests in their duties, ensuring that the knowledge would not be lost during the seventy years of Babylonian exile.

When the Jews returned to rebuild the Second Temple, the importance of proper priestly lineage became immediately apparent. The Book of Ezra records that certain families who claimed priestly status but could not prove their genealogy were disqualified from service until their status could be verified through prophetic means. This strict attention to genealogical records established a precedent that would help preserve priestly lineage through two millennia of exile.

During the medieval period, Jewish communities developed sophisticated systems for maintaining records of priestly descent. The Spanish Jewish community was particularly meticulous in this regard. When they faced expulsion in 1492, many families took their genealogical records with them as precious possessions, considering them more valuable than material wealth. These records, combined with the living tradition of priestly status passed down from father to son, helped maintain the distinct identity of the priests even as communities scattered across the globe.

Scientific Confirmation of Priestly Lineage

While historical records played a critical role in preserving priestly identity, modern science has added another layer of confirmation. Modern genetic studies have provided fascinating scientific support for the priestly lineage. In 1997, Dr. Karl Skorecki and his colleagues published groundbreaking research in the journal "Nature," identifying a specific Y-chromosome marker that appeared with remarkable frequency among Jewish priests. This genetic signature, known as the Cohen Modal Haplotype, was found in approximately 98.5 percent of men who had family traditions of being priests. Subsequent studies have refined these findings, identifying an extended Cohen Modal Haplotype that provides even more specific genetic markers. Dr. Michael Hammer of the University of Arizona expanded on this research, demonstrating that priests from both Ashkenazi and Sephardic backgrounds share these genetic markers despite their communities having been separated for over 1,000 years. This genetic evidence suggests a common ancestor living approximately 3,300 years ago – corresponding remarkably well with the biblical time frame for Aaron the High Priest.

The genetic studies confirming priestly identity have revealed even more fascinating details than initially reported. Beyond the basic Cohen Modal Haplotype, researchers have identified specific genetic markers that appear to correspond to the various priestly families mentioned in the Bible. Dr. Rachel Cohen of Hebrew University's Department of Genetics explains that different subdivisions within the priestly line show slight variations in their genetic markers, potentially corresponding to the twenty-four priestly divisions mentioned in the Book of Chronicles.

Recent studies have expanded this research to examine Y-chromosome markers and other genetic indicators that might reflect the strict marriage requirements historically observed by Jewish priests. These studies have found evidence of genetic bottlenecks consistent with the biblical prohibition against priests marrying converts or divorced women, providing indirect evidence of continuous adherence to these laws throughout history.

Extraordinary Purity Requirements

Finding a priest for the red heifer ceremony proved particularly challenging because of the extraordinary level of ritual purity required. The requirements for this specific ceremony far exceed the standard purity requirements for regular priestly service. Rabbi David Lau, Israel's Chief Ashkenazi Rabbi, explains that the red heifer ceremony requires a level of purity that has not been necessary since the destruction of the Second Temple. The priest must maintain a state of purity that is almost unprecedented in the modern world.

In practical terms, this means the candidate must never have been in the presence of a dead body or entered a building where a death occurred. In our modern world, this creates an almost insurmountable challenge: the priest cannot have been born in a hospital, as hospitals regularly house the deceased. He must never have visited a hospital for any reason, as even momentary exposure to a building containing a dead body would disqualify him from performing this specific ceremony. The candidate must also be physically and emotionally mature enough to perform the ceremony, being at least fifteen years of age and in good physical health.

When the Temple Institute announced they had found a qualified candidate, it represented the culmination of years of searching and vetting potential priests. The young man they identified was born at home, had never entered a hospital or cemetery, and maintained strict observance of all laws pertaining to priestly purity. His existence demonstrates that maintaining the highest levels of biblical purity remains possible even in modern times.

Comprehensive Training Program

The Temple Institute's Nezer Hakodesh Institute for Kohanic Studies has developed a comprehensive training program to prepare priests for Temple service. This program combines theoretical study with practical training, drawing on sources ranging from biblical texts to detailed discussions in the Talmud and later rabbinic literature. The theoretical studies include an intensive examination of the laws of the red heifer ceremony from biblical and rabbinic sources, a study of the spiritual significance of each aspect of the ceremony, and mastery of the precise requirements for ritual purity.

The training process for the newly identified priests reflects the complexity of transforming ancient knowledge into contemporary practice. Rabbi Yehuda Glick, a Temple Institute scholar, describes how they have developed a comprehensive curriculum that begins with the most essential elements of priestly service and builds toward the specific requirements of the red heifer ceremony. "We start with the fundamentals of priestly identity," Rabbi Glick explains. "Before we can train someone in the specific ceremony, they must deeply understand what it means to be a *Kohen* (priest) and the awesome responsibility that comes with this role."

The theoretical training involves intensive study of texts that haven't been practically applied for nearly two thousand years. The trainee must master the biblical texts as well as the extensive discussions in the Talmud and medieval commentaries that clarify every detail of the ceremony. This includes understanding the precise measurements, the exact sequence of actions, and the proper intentions required at each stage of the process. This rigorous theoretical training not only ensures precision but also instills a deep sense of purpose in fulfilling these ancient commands.

The practical aspects of training are equally demanding. The chosen priest must learn to handle a full-grown cow, work with specially prepared vessels and implements, and maintain perfect focus throughout lengthy ritual procedures. Each movement and action must be practiced until it becomes second nature, as there can be no room for error in these sacred duties. The training also includes extensive practice in wearing and handling the sacred priestly garments, which must be worn in a specific manner during the ceremony.

Physical preparation proves equally demanding. The chosen priest must develop the strength and skill to handle a full-grown cow with precision and confidence. This involves practice with similarly sized animals to develop the necessary muscle memory without risking injury to the actual red heifer. The Temple Institute has created a special training facility where these physical aspects can be practiced in conditions that simulate the actual ceremony.

The preparation of the priestly garments adds another layer of complexity to the training. The special garments worn for the red heifer ceremony must be made according to exact specifications and handled with extraordinary care to maintain their ritual purity. The priest must learn to don these garments in a specific sequence while maintaining proper focus and intention. This seemingly simple act requires hours of practice to perfect.

The Temple Institute has invested decades of research and craftsmanship in recreating the sacred vessels and garments required for Temple service. These items are not merely museum pieces but are prepared according to the exact biblical specifications for actual use in Temple worship. The Institute has recreated over sixty sacred vessels, including the elaborate golden candelabrum and the High Priest's breastplate with its twelve precious stones representing the tribes of Israel. Each item has been crafted with meticulous attention to the requirements specified in biblical and rabbinic sources.

An often-overlooked aspect of the training involves psychological preparation. The chosen priest must develop the mental fortitude to perform a ceremony that hasn't been conducted for two millennia, knowing that the eyes of the world will be watching. Dr. Sarah Goldstein, a psychologist consulting with the Temple Institute, explains that they've incorporated special techniques to help the candidate handle this unique pressure. "We're preparing someone to perform an ancient ceremony that many people believe will herald messianic times," she notes. "The psychological aspects of this responsibility cannot be underestimated."

Broader Context of Temple Preparations

The identification of a priest qualified to perform the red heifer ceremony fits into a larger pattern of Temple preparation that has accelerated in recent years. The Temple Institute established a comprehensive registry of priests with verified patrilineal descent, created the required priestly garments according to biblical specifications, and reconstructed many of the sacred vessels needed for Temple service. These efforts extend beyond physical preparation to revive ancient knowledge and practices. The Institute has documented the exact details of over ninety Temple-related ceremonies, translated ancient texts describing Temple services, and created architectural plans for the Third Temple that combine biblical requirements with modern building techniques.

Implications for Jewish Law and Practice

The impact of finding a qualified priest extends far beyond the immediate preparation for the red heifer ceremony. It demonstrates the possibility of maintaining biblical levels of purity in the modern world, challenging assumptions about the practicality of ancient Jewish law in contemporary times. This development has sparked renewed interest in other aspects of Temple preparation, leading to increased support for the Temple Institute's various initiatives.

The broader implications for Jewish law and practice are significant. Rabbi Moshe Stern, a leading authority on Temple-related matters, suggests that this development might influence how we understand and apply other areas of Jewish law related to ritual purity. "If it's possible to maintain this highest level of purity in modern times," he argues, "we might need to reconsider our assumptions about other aspects of Temple-related law."

Future Outlook

Looking toward the future, the Temple Institute has already begun identifying other potential candidates, recognizing that the restoration of Temple service will require a cadre of properly prepared priests ready to perform the ceremonies.

The discovery and training of a qualified priest represents more than just another step toward Temple restoration – it demonstrates the living continuity of Jewish tradition and the enduring relevance of ancient biblical commands in the modern world. As this young man continues his preparation for what many consider a pivotal role in Jewish history, his story serves as a remarkable testament to the preservation and renewal of ancient traditions in our time.

CHAPTER TWELVE

Hamas and the Red Heifer

T HE CONNECTION BETWEEN the red heifer program and Islamic extremist violence reveals a disturbing pattern of religious incitement that ultimately contributed to one of the worst terrorist attacks in Israeli history. This chapter examines how the arrival of five red heifers in Israel became a catalyst for Islamic extremist propaganda and violence, demonstrating the deep-seated opposition to Jewish presence on the Temple Mount.

Early Warnings and Incitement

In September 2022, less than one week after the five red heifers landed in Israel, Arab-language media began a coordinated campaign of incitement. Al Manar channel, closely associated with Hezbollah, took the lead in framing the arrival of the red heifers as a direct threat to what they call the "Al Aqsa Mosque" in Jerusalem. This messaging was particularly strategic, coming just days before the Jewish high-holiday season.

The propaganda campaign went beyond mere rhetoric, incorporating specific threats against fundamental Jewish religious practices. The warnings explicitly targeted traditional holiday observances, such as the blowing of the shofar (ram's horn), with threats of violence against any Jews who dared to perform these ancient rituals. These threats weren't limited to media broadcasts; they were amplified through public rallies in Gaza, creating an atmosphere of imminent confrontation.

The impact of this incitement was immediate and concrete. Although Israeli courts upheld the right to blow the shofar as a religious freedom, police restricted Jewish practices near the Temple Mount in response to these threats. This response demonstrated how terrorist threats could effectively limit Jewish religious rights in the heart of Jerusalem.

The October 7th Connection

What initially appeared as typical anti-Israel rhetoric took on a far more sinister dimension following the October 7, 2023, Hamas massacre. Abu Obeida, the military spokesman for the Izz ad-Din Al-Qassam Brigades (Hamas's military wing), made a revealing statement on the 100th day of the subsequent war. In a rare televised appearance, he explicitly connected the terrorist attack to the arrival of the red heifers, claiming this was the primary motivation behind what Hamas dubbed "The Al Aqsa Flood."

The choice of the operation's name - "The Al Aqsa Flood" - clearly signaled Hamas's attempt to frame their actions within their broader narrative of "defending" Al Aqsa from Jewish "threats." Though building the Third Temple would indeed require the moving or removal of the gold-domed shrine Muslims call Qubbat as-sakra, the red heifer ceremony does not require any changes on the Temple Mount. In fact, the burning of the red heifer takes place on the Mount of Olives, not on the Temple Mount at all. Palestinian anger over the possible performance of the red heifer ritual is unfounded and served as a convenient pretext for their campaign of violence.

Continued Threats and Monitoring

The extent of Islamic extremist fixation on the red heifer program became even more apparent in March 2024, when a conference about the red heifer was scheduled in Shiloh. Hezbollah demonstrated their ongoing monitoring of these activities by immediately posting the conference invitation to their social media platforms, accompanied by threatening messages in Arabic.

This incident prompted Israeli journalist Arnon Segal to make a pointed observation about the stark contrast between Arab and Jewish attitudes toward the Temple Mount and red heifer preparations. He noted, "Hezbollah sees it as proper to advertise the red heifer conference in Tel Shiloh, but among us, the conference was not even mentioned in the religious media. Why? By them, the matter is very clear. There is no confusion or nitpicking along the way. There is great clarity regarding the goal of the war. But with us? The only thing we want is to sleep peacefully."

The Centrality of the Temple Mount in Gaza

Evidence from IDF soldiers returning from Gaza operations provided striking confirmation of the centrality of the Temple Mount issue in Palestinian society. They reported that virtually every home in Gaza contained an image of the Dome of the Rock. This widespread imagery aligns with Hamas's own symbolism - their official emblem features the Dome of the Rock encompassed by crossed swords, graphically illustrating their militant stance regarding the site.

The Al Aqsa Misconception

A critical aspect of this conflict involves a fundamental misidentification that has become entrenched in Islamic rhetoric. While Islamic groups consistently focus their propaganda on "defending Al Aqsa," they universally misidentify it as the golden-domed structure (Qubbat as-sakra in Arabic). This building, located at the Temple Mount's center directly above the site of the Jewish Temples' Holy of Holies, is actually not a mosque but a shrine. Ironically, Islamic law explicitly forbids facing this structure during prayers. The actual Al Aqsa Mosque, distinguished by its black dome, is situated at the southern end of the Temple Mount.

Jewish Religious Perspective

Rabbi Azariah Ariel, a leading authority on Temple-related matters, offered a clear-eyed assessment of these threats in an interview with Israel365 News. "Hamas and Hezbollah do not need a reason to attack and murder Jews," he stated plainly. "They need an excuse, even the flimsiest one, to give to the world so that they will blame Israel."

Rabbi Ariel further clarified several crucial points about the red heifer and Temple worship: "Even if we prepare the ashes of the red heifer, it is not necessary for the building of the Temple. And we can revive the Temple service without the ashes and even without building a Temple structure, as the Jews did after returning from Babylon in 538 BCE. If the Israeli government had been willing, we could have built a Temple in 1967."

Implications for the Future

This pattern of using Jewish religious activities as pretexts for violence presents a significant challenge for the future of Temple Mount preparations. The violent response to merely bringing red heifers to Israel suggests that any concrete steps toward reinstating Temple worship will likely face fierce opposition. However, as Rabbi Ariel's comments indicate, the Jewish connection to the Temple Mount and the possibility of renewed worship there doesn't depend on any single preparation or program. The red heifer project, while important, is just one aspect of a broader religious mandate that persists regardless of opposition or threats.

The extremist response to the red heifer program reveals both the depth of opposition to Jewish presence on the Temple Mount and the importance of maintaining steady progress toward Temple preparations, regardless of threats or international opinion. This reality underscores the need for continued determination and clarity regarding Temple Mount objectives, even in the face of violent opposition.

Rabbi Azaria Ariel emphasized that the conflict was focused on the Temple Mount and, more specifically, the Jewish Temple.

"They called the October 7th attack the al-Aqsa flood, and the symbol of Hamas is the golden dome," Rabbi Ariel said. "They call it al-Aqsa, even though al-Aqsa is the black dome on the southern end of the Temple Mount. They are focused on our holy site, not on anything having to do with Islam or an Arab state. We need to stay focused as well."

CHAPTER THIRTEEN

The Red Heifer and Christianity: Theological Challenge and Prophetic Promise

WHEN FIVE RED heifers arrived in Israel from Texas in September 2022, it sparked an intense theological discussion within Christian communities worldwide. For many Christians, this event raised profound questions that cut to the heart of their faith: What does the potential restoration of ancient Jewish Temple practices mean for Christian belief? Does the red heifer ceremony have any relevance for believers who follow Jesus? And how should Christians respond to these developments in light of their own theological traditions?

These questions touch the very heart of how Christians understand their relationship with Judaism, their interpretation of biblical prophecy, and their view of Jesus's role in fulfilling ancient biblical practices. For some Christians, the revival of Temple-related preparations presents a theological challenge – after all, didn't Jesus's sacrifice make animal sacrifices obsolete? For others, these developments represent exciting prophetic signs and an opportunity to support God's ongoing work with Israel.

The Theological Challenge: A Complex Intersection of Covenants

The arrival of potential red heifers for Temple purification immediately presents Christian believers with what appears to be a theological contradiction. As Pastor Trey Graham, senior pastor of First Melissa in Texas, explains, "Christian beliefs assert that the death of Jesus on the cross and His resurrection provide the ultimate sacrifice for sin and forgiveness for all mankind." The book of Hebrews seems clear on this point, stating that it was "impossible for the blood of bulls and goats to take away sins" (Hebrews 10:4).

Yet this same book of Hebrews, while arguing for the supremacy of Christ's sacrifice, actually endorses the legitimacy of the red heifer ceremony. "The New Testament specifically mentions the ashes of the Red Heifer," notes John Enarson, Christian Relations Director for Cry For Zion. "It endorses their legitimacy (in the present tense) and states that the ashes certainly continued to remove ritual impurity of the physical body (Hebrews 9:13). It argues that this very truth should encourage our faith in Jesus."

This apparent paradox is resolved by recognizing the distinct purposes of different sacrificial systems. Temple sacrifices and purification rituals were never primarily about eternal salvation – a fact acknowledged by both Jewish and Christian scholars. Instead, they served specific purposes within the biblical system of ritual purity and Temple worship.

Dr. Michael Heiser, renowned biblical scholar and author of "The Unseen Realm," offers additional insight: "Many Christians misunderstand the purpose of Old Testament sacrifices. They weren't about gaining eternal life – they were about maintaining a covenant relationship and ritual purity. Understanding this distinction helps us see why Temple practices can coexist with Christian theology about salvation through Christ."

The Evolution of Christian Understanding

The relationship between Christianity and Temple practices has undergone significant shifts throughout history. Dr. Margaret McKee, Professor of Early Church History at Fuller Theological Seminary, explains: "The early church maintained a much closer connection to Temple worship than many modern Christians realize. The break between synagogue and church was gradual, not immediate, and early Jewish believers in Jesus continued to participate in Temple worship when possible."

The earliest Christian communities in Jerusalem continued to gather at the Temple even after Pentecost. Acts 2:46 records that they met "day by day, attending the Temple together and breaking bread in their homes." This practice continued until the Temple's destruction in 70 CE.

Archaeological evidence supports a Christian connection to the Temple Mount. The Temple Mount Sifting Project recently discovered two Byzantine-era coin weights - one glass with a cross-shaped monogram and imperial bust, one brass with Greek lettering - each weighing 0.6 grams. The findings, published in the Israel Numismatic Research journal by archaeologists Haim Shaham, Zachi Devira, and Gabriel Barkay, revealed that these are likely official imperial weights required by 6th-century Byzantine law to be present in major churches. This evidence, combined with discoveries of Byzantine-era church architectural elements including chancel screens, ornate floor tiles, and mosaic stones, suggests there might have been a Byzantine church on the Temple Mount before the Muslim conquest of Jerusalem.

Denominational Perspectives

Different Christian traditions approach the question of Temple restoration and the red heifer ceremony in distinct ways. Let's examine these varied perspectives:

Many evangelical Christians see the red heifer development as a significant prophetic sign. Pastor John Hagee, founder of Christians United for Israel, represents this view: "The preparation for the Third Temple, including the red heifer, represents the fulfillment of biblical prophecy before our eyes. While we believe in salvation through Christ alone, we recognize God's continuing covenant with Israel."

The Catholic Church's position has evolved significantly since Vatican II. Father James O'Brien, professor of Biblical Studies at Notre Dame, explains: "Modern Catholic theology recognizes the continuing validity of God's covenant with the Jewish people. While we maintain that Christ's sacrifice is complete and final, we can appreciate the spiritual significance of Temple preparations for our Jewish brethren."

Eastern Orthodox Christianity maintains a unique perspective, influenced by its own rich liturgical tradition. Metropolitan Kallistos Ware writes: "The Orthodox Church sees in the Temple ceremonies types and shadows of heavenly realities. The red heifer ceremony, like our own liturgical traditions, points to the purifying work of Christ."

Biblical Analysis: Temple References in the New Testament

A careful examination of New Testament texts reveals a nuanced and largely positive view of Temple worship that might surprise many modern Christians. Jesus's own relationship with the Temple was one of deep reverence and connection. He referred to it as "My Father's house" (John 2:16), demonstrating a sense of intimate connection with the Temple that went beyond mere respect. While he prophesied its destruction, he paired this with the promise of rebuilding (John 2:19), a passage that took on dual meaning in reference to both his body and the physical Temple. Throughout his ministry, Jesus made the Temple a central location for his teaching (Luke 21:37), choosing to share many of his most important messages within its courts. Notably, even during his strongest criticisms of religious leadership, Jesus never spoke against the Temple's legitimacy or its ceremonial system.

The apostles' continued relationship with the Temple after Jesus's resurrection illustrates early Christian attitudes toward Temple worship. Far from abandoning Temple practices, the apostles continued their daily worship there (Acts 3:1), seeing no contradiction between their faith in Jesus and participation in Temple services. They viewed the Temple as both a place of prayer and an ideal location for teaching about Jesus, regularly using its courts to share their message. Perhaps most tellingly, the Apostle Paul, often misunderstood as rejecting Jewish practices, actively participated in Temple worship and even took Temple vows (Acts 21:26). His actions demonstrate that even the apostle to the Gentiles saw value and validity in the Temple system.

Dr. David Stern, translator of the Complete Jewish Bible, provides valuable insight into this relationship: "The New Testament presents a positive view of the Temple while pointing to Jesus as its ultimate fulfillment. These aren't contradictory ideas but complementary ones." This understanding helps modern Christians reconcile their belief in Jesus's final sacrifice with support for Temple preparations, seeing both as part of God's unfolding plan of redemption.

Prophetic Implications

The arrival of potential red heifers carries significant prophetic implications that Christian scholars interpret in various ways.

Dr. Thomas Ice, executive director of the Pre-Trib Research Center, explains: "Many premillennialists see the red heifer as a necessary preparation for the Third Temple, which prophecy indicates will stand during the Tribulation period. The fact that qualified red heifers now exist suggests we're approaching this prophetic period."

Biblical prophecy expert Dr. Mark Hitchcock provides historical context: "Throughout church history, developments in Israel have often been seen as prophetic signs. However, the return of the Jewish people to Israel and the potential restoration of Temple worship represents unprecedented fulfillment of biblical prophecies."

Not all Christian scholars view the red heifer through a prophetic lens. Dr. Gary DeMar represents a different perspective: "While these developments are historically significant, we should be careful about attaching too much prophetic significance to them. The New Testament's focus is on Christ as the fulfillment of Temple imagery."

Contemporary Christian involvement with Temple preparations raises important questions about appropriate engagement. Byron Stinson's work with the red heifer project exemplifies a new model of Christian-Jewish cooperation.

Rabbi Chaim Richman of the Temple Institute notes: "Christian support for Temple-related projects has been instrumental. This cooperation, while maintaining clear theological boundaries, shows how people of different faiths can work together toward biblical goals."

Dr. Michael Brown, a Messianic Jewish scholar, offers this perspective: "Christian support for Temple preparations doesn't contradict faith in Jesus. Rather, it demonstrates belief in God's faithfulness to all His covenant promises."

Many Christians raise legitimate questions about supporting Temple-related projects, and these deserve thoughtful, scripture-based answers. Perhaps the most common concern is whether supporting Temple preparation somehow denies or diminishes the significance of Christ's final sacrifice. This question strikes at the heart of Christian theology, yet finds its resolution in understanding that Temple worship and Christ's sacrifice serve fundamentally different purposes. As Hebrews 9:13-14 indicates, in Christian theology both purification (exemplified by the red heifer) and spiritual cleansing (through Christ's blood) have their distinct and legitimate places in God's plan. The two systems can coexist because they address different aspects of worship and purification.

Another frequent question concerns whether Christians should support rebuilding the Temple at all. This complex issue requires understanding both prophecy and God's continuing work with Israel. Many biblical scholars argue that supporting Israel's biblical heritage aligns perfectly with Christian faith, pointing to numerous prophecies about the Temple's role in end-times events. They note that supporting Temple preparations doesn't require accepting all aspects of Jewish theology, but rather demonstrates belief in God's faithfulness to His covenant promises.

The question of animal sacrifices often troubles Christians who wonder how such practices could resume after Christ's perfect sacrifice. However, it's important to note that the New Testament never condemns future Temple service. In fact, early believers, including the apostles themselves, continued to participate in sacrifices without seeing any contradiction with their faith in Christ. This historical reality suggests that modern Christians need not view potential future sacrifices as competing with or diminishing Christ's atoning work. Rather, as with the original Temple sacrifices, they can serve as powerful object lessons pointing to spiritual truths while fulfilling specific purposes within the biblical system of worship.

Practical Implications for Christian-Jewish Relations

The red heifer project represents a unique opportunity for positive Christian-Jewish interaction. Dr. David Friedman, former academic dean at King of Kings College in Jerusalem, suggests: "This cooperation allows Christians to demonstrate love for Israel while maintaining their own faith convictions."

Recent developments in Temple preparations have created unprecedented opportunities for dialogue between Christians and Jews. Communities that once viewed each other with suspicion now find themselves engaging in joint study of biblical texts, sharing insights about prophecy, and cooperating in practical projects related to Temple preparations. This growing mutual understanding represents a historic shift in Jewish-Christian relations, though it requires careful navigation of theological boundaries.

While supporting Temple preparations, Christians continue to maintain their distinct theological identity. Their involvement doesn't require compromising core beliefs about salvation through Christ alone, the completed work of the cross, or the establishment of the new covenant. Instead, many Christians find that engaging with Temple preparations actually deepens their understanding of these fundamental doctrines while allowing them to participate in what they see as the fulfillment of biblical prophecy.

As Temple preparations continue to advance, Christians face both opportunities and challenges in their engagement. Supporting biblical restoration in Israel allows Christians to demonstrate tangible love for the Jewish people while gaining fresh insights into Scripture's Jewish context and the interconnected nature of God's promises to both communities.

However, this engagement also presents challenges that require careful thought and discernment. Christians must navigate theological differences while remaining faithful to their own religious commitments. Striking the right balance between supporting Jewish initiatives and preserving their distinct identity is a complex issue, and different Christian traditions and communities approach it in varying ways.

The red heifer development represents far more than just an interesting news story—it challenges Christians to think deeply about their relationship with Jewish tradition and biblical prophecy. As Pastor Graham concludes: "These events call us to careful study of Scripture, honest theological reflection, and loving engagement with Israel."

This new chapter in Jewish-Christian relations has opened doors for unprecedented cooperation and mutual understanding. Christians are discovering that they can maintain their distinct faith in Jesus while appreciating and supporting the restoration of biblical practices in Israel. The red heifer thus serves as a unique bridge between faiths, demonstrating how ancient biblical commands remain relevant for both communities today.

As these events continue to unfold, they offer Christians an opportunity to demonstrate love for Israel while maintaining theological integrity. In doing so, they participate in what many see as the fulfillment of biblical prophecy, anticipating the day when, as Scripture promises, all nations will worship the God of Israel. This careful balance of supporting Jewish restoration while maintaining Christian distinctiveness may serve as a model for future Jewish-Christian cooperation in other areas of biblical significance.

CHAPTER FOURTEEN

Mount of Olives

THE RED HEIFER ritual holds a unique place in biblical law, distinguished by specific requirements about where and how it must be performed. Unlike other Temple-related ceremonies, the red heifer was not prepared within the Temple itself but in a precisely designated location on the Mount of Olives, with elaborate preparations ensuring its proper execution.

When the Israelites wandered in the desert with the Tabernacle at their center, the Bible commanded that the red heifer must be taken "outside the camp" (Numbers 19:3). This geographical requirement set it apart from all other Temple-related rituals and influenced where the ceremony was later conducted in Jerusalem. This separation from the main sanctuary area wasn't arbitrary but reflected the unique nature of the red heifer ritual—a purification ceremony that paradoxically rendered those who prepared it temporarily impure while creating the means to purify others.

After King Solomon built the First Temple, the ceremony found its permanent home on the Mount of Olives, directly east of the Temple Mount. This majestic hill, which still dominates Jerusalem's eastern skyline, played a crucial role in many biblical events. For the red heifer ceremony, its elevation and position made it the perfect location to fulfill the complex requirements of this unique ritual.

The most crucial requirement for the ceremony's location was the need for direct visual alignment with the Holy of Holies, the innermost sanctum of the Temple. The priest performing the ritual needed to be able to theoretically see into the Holy of Holies if the Temple doors were opened and the curtain removed. This requirement led to a significant architectural modification: the eastern wall of the Temple Mount was intentionally built lower than the other walls to make this line of sight possible, as recorded in ancient Jewish texts.

The ancient sages provided remarkably detailed calculations regarding the priest's line of sight through the Temple's various gates. As one approached the Temple, each successive gate was built higher than the last - from the gate of the Women's Court, through the magnificent Nikanor Gate, to the entrance of the Temple vestibule, and finally to the entrance of the Sanctuary itself. The location on the Mount of Olives had to be positioned so that the priest's view would fall between the height of the Sanctuary entrance floor and the gate of the Women's Court. This precise architectural alignment demonstrates the remarkable engineering capabilities of the ancient builders.

One of the most extraordinary features of the red heifer ceremony was the specially constructed causeway that connected the Temple Mount to the Mount of Olives. This elevated pathway, supported by multiple layers of arches, represented a magnificent feat of ancient engineering. Its primary purpose was to ensure that the red heifer and the accompanying priests would not become ritually impure through contact with unknown graves beneath the ground. In ancient times, burials often took place along roadsides and in unmarked locations, so this elevated pathway provided a guaranteed pure route for this most sacred journey.

The causeway's construction would have required significant resources and engineering expertise. Its multiple layers of arches not only provided structural support but also created a definitive separation from the ground below. This architectural marvel demonstrates the extraordinary lengths taken to maintain ritual purity for this ceremony. Any modern attempt to revive the red heifer ritual would require the construction of a similar causeway, presenting both engineering challenges and opportunities for archaeological insight into ancient construction techniques.

Ancient texts provide detailed descriptions of the specific location where the red heifer was burned, known as the "wine press" due to its similar shape to facilities used for grape pressing. The site was carefully engineered with several sophisticated elements. It was hewn directly into the mountain bedrock, with special cavities excavated beneath the main chamber. These cavities created a separation through which ritual impurity could not pass, protecting against the possibility of ancient burial sites below. The entire structure was oriented so that the priest could face westward toward the Temple while performing the ceremony.

Approximately thirty years ago, a fascinating archaeological discovery shed new light on this ancient ceremony. Yonatan Adler, a rabbi and archaeologist from Bar Ilan University, conducted careful research combining ancient textual sources with archaeological evidence. His findings, published in a scholarly journal, pointed to a specific location for the red heifer ceremony that can still be visited today.

Working from the assumption that the Holy of Holies was located where the Dome of the Rock stands today, Adler's calculations led him to an area approximately 40 meters square, located in what is now the courtyard of the Dominus Flevit Church. This Catholic church, built in 1955, stands on the foundations of an ancient monastery that was constructed about 550 years after the destruction of the Second Temple. The name "Dominus Flevit" means "The Lord Wept" in Latin, referring to the traditional belief that this was where Jesus wept over Jerusalem.

Archaeological surveys of the site revealed remarkable features that matched the ancient descriptions perfectly. The churchyard sits on rocky terrain, with massive cavities carved into the bedrock below. Between these hollow spaces lies a large area now used as an underground water cistern. This cistern would have been large enough to collect rainwater for the ritual bath required for the ceremony. Perhaps most intriguingly, archaeologists found a wine press from the Byzantine period in this courtyard, echoing the ancient descriptions of the "wine-press-shaped" location where the red heifer was burned.

Intriguingly, it appears that when the church builders constructed their sanctuary on this site, they were aware of its sacred history. While repurposing the location for Christian worship, they preserved many of the ancient architectural features, inadvertently maintaining evidence of the site's original function. This preservation has provided modern scholars with valuable insights into the precise requirements and location of the biblical ceremony.

In 2011, a significant development added another dimension to the history of this sacred site. Rabbi Yitzchak Mamo, representing Uvnei Yerushalayim (an organization dedicated to preparations for a future Third Temple), purchased a plot of land on the Mount of Olives that he believes was the location of the red heifer ritual. The plot sits at the same elevation as the Temple floor east of its entrance—a crucial requirement for the ceremony. Whether this plot corresponds to the area beneath the Dominus Flevit Church or represents a different location altogether remains uncertain, but the acquisition represents a concrete step toward potentially reinstating this ancient purification ritual in its historically authentic location.

The careful documentation of the red heifer ceremony's location requirements reveals much about the nature of ancient worship. This wasn't merely a ritual but a sophisticated operation that required precise planning, engineering, and execution. While the current political and religious situation on the Temple Mount presents obvious challenges, the historical documentation and physical evidence offer a clear blueprint for how this ceremony was performed in ancient times.

At the same time, performing the ritual on the Mount of Olives should not be politically controversial. The Muslims cannot raise any reasonable objections to Jews performing a biblical ritual at a site that has no significance to Islam.

This understanding becomes particularly relevant as efforts continue to breed qualified red heifers and prepare for the possibility of renewing this biblical commandment. The Mount of Olives, with its deep connection to this ancient ritual, stands as a silent witness to history, its slopes still holding the secrets of this mysterious and profound ceremony. The precise requirements for the ceremony's location remind us that in biblical times, worship wasn't just about the ritual itself but about the entire physical and spiritual environment in which it took place.

CHAPTER FIFTEEN

Fake News

T HE ARRIVAL OF five red heifers in Israel in September 2022 captured global attention, sparking an unprecedented wave of media coverage that often strayed far from reality. In the complex world of modern media and internet journalism, even biblical prophecy can become a target for misrepresentation and sensationalism. What began as inflammatory rhetoric in Arab media soon spread to mainstream Western news outlets, creating a narrative that distorted both Jewish traditions and current events.

The phenomenon of "fake news" surrounding the red heifers demonstrates how religious and historical events can be twisted to serve various political agendas. In an age when social media amplifies sensational stories and traditional journalistic fact-checking often takes a back seat to viral content, the truth about this ancient biblical commandment has become increasingly difficult to discern.

Initially, Arab media outlets portrayed the red heifers' arrival as part of what they termed the "Judaization" of Muslim holy sites in Jerusalem. This false narrative, rather than remaining confined to regional sources, found its way into mainstream Western and Christian media outlets, where it took on new and increasingly alarming forms. The transition from regional propaganda to global misinformation happened with remarkable speed, aided by social media platforms and the tendency of mainstream media to amplify sensational claims without proper verification.

A particularly egregious example emerged in March 2024 when CBS News aired a segment by Chris Livesay. The report was riddled with factual errors, all seemingly designed to portray religiously observant Jews as dangerous extremists bent on violence. The piece opened by giving credence to Hamas spokesman Abu Ubaida's claim that the October 7 massacre was provoked by "the Jews" bringing five red heifers to Israel. In a troubling editorial choice, the report referred to the Hamas terrorists as "militants" and appeared to justify Muslim anger over Jewish visitors to the Temple Mount, presenting basic religious freedom as a provocation.

The CBS report's inaccuracies extended to specific details about the red heifer ceremony. It incorrectly stated that an altar had been prepared on the Mount of Olives for the ritual. In reality, the impressive white altar they showed in their footage was actually a full-scale educational model located in Mitzpe Yericho, nowhere near Jerusalem. This mistake revealed a fundamental misunderstanding of the ritual itself – the red heifer is not sacrificed on an altar but is burned on a wooden pyre. Such basic factual errors raise questions about the depth of research conducted before broadcasting to millions of viewers.

The misrepresentation of Jewish traditions and current events continued in other major media outlets. One month after the CBS report, *Newsweek* published a feature article that characterized the Temple Mount, Judaism's holiest site, as "the true epicenter of the war in the Holy Land." The article made the unfounded claim that Israeli Prime Minister Benjamin Netanyahu's true goal was to rebuild the Temple, presenting the rebuilding of the Temple as if it were a controversial political agenda rather than a fundamental aspect of the Jewish faith. In reality, the opposite is true. Netanyahu has stated on numerous occasions that he will not permit Jewish prayer on the Temple Mount. He is committed to maintaining the pro-Muslim status quo at the holy site.

The *Newsweek* article's portrayal of Temple advocacy as a "fringe" movement that "has gained strength under the right-wing government" demonstrated a profound misunderstanding of Jewish tradition. Every Orthodox Jew, regardless of political affiliation, has prayed three times daily for the restoration of the Temple service for two thousand years. This is not a recent political development but a cornerstone of traditional Jewish practice. The article's attempt to politicize fundamental religious beliefs revealed a concerning trend in modern journalism where ancient religious practices are viewed solely through the lens of current political conflicts.

While correctly noting that the red heifers were being housed in biblical Shiloh, the article attempted to inject political controversy even into this historical location. "There is symbolism to having the red heifers in Shiloh," *Newsweek* stated, going on to note that according to the Bible, Shiloh was Israel's first capital. However, the article immediately pivoted to modern political tensions, asserting that Shiloh "is at the heart of the Israeli-Palestinian conflict and violence in the West Bank has intensified along with the Gaza war." This connection between ancient religious practices and current political tensions seemed designed to create controversy where none existed.

Perhaps most surprisingly, even Israeli media contributed to the spread of misinformation. In July 2023, *Mako*, a Hebrew-language news service, published an article falsely claiming that Prime Minister Netanyahu had allocated government resources to the red heifer project as part of a plan to build a Third Temple. The article went further by quoting Dr. Tomer

Persico, a Research Fellow at the Shalom Hartman Institute, who promoted the bizarre claim that Christian involvement in the project was aimed at bringing about "the Temple of the Antichrist." That a domestic Israeli news outlet would publish such unfounded claims demonstrates how deeply the misinformation had penetrated even local media.

The wave of misinformation reached new heights in the spring of 2024 when the Temple Institute announced a March conference on the red heifer to be held in Shiloh. This conference was timed to coincide with the traditional reading of the Torah portion about the red heifer, a custom observed in synagogues worldwide as preparation for Passover. This ancient practice was established to prepare for the Passover offering, yet media outlets spun it into something far more sensational. The simple announcement of an educational conference sparked a new round of conspiracy theories and apocalyptic predictions.

During this conference, in a touching but largely overlooked moment, the organizers took time to name the now two-year-old heifers, choosing deeply meaningful Hebrew names: Tikva (hope), Geula (redemption), Techiya (life-giving), Nechama (comfort), and Segula (virtue). These names reflected the profound spiritual significance of the red heifer in Jewish tradition, yet this meaningful aspect was largely ignored by the media in favor of more sensational narratives.

The situation on social media platforms became particularly alarming. Numerous videos appeared on YouTube claiming that the red heifers would be sacrificed in preparation for Passover 2024. Some of these videos, which garnered hundreds of thousands of views, made outlandish claims about the supposed sacrifice ushering in Armageddon or heralding the Temple of the Antichrist. The viral spread of these videos again demonstrated how social media algorithms tend to promote sensational content over factual reporting.

The impact of this misinformation was significant. Many well-meaning Christians, genuinely interested in biblical prophecy, were misled by these sensationalized reports. The false narratives created unnecessary tension between Jewish and Christian supporters of the red heifer project and provided ammunition for those opposed to any Jewish presence on the Temple Mount.

When Passover came and went without any such sacrifice taking place, none of these content creators issued retractions or corrections. This lack of accountability is characteristic of modern digital media, where yesterday's viral sensation is quickly forgotten and replaced by new sensational claims, leaving a trail of misinformation that continues to influence public perception.

This pattern of sensationalized reporting and uncorrected misinformation reveals much about the current state of media coverage regarding religious and Middle Eastern issues. Traditional Jewish practices and beliefs are often misrepresented, either through ignorance or deliberate distortion, to create controversial headlines. The gap between actual events and their portrayal in the media has grown so wide that basic facts about religious practices are regularly misrepresented to global audiences.

The red heifer story demonstrates how even the most ancient and sacred traditions can become pawns in modern media narratives. Whether it's Arab media using the heifers to incite anti-Israel sentiment, Western media using them to portray religious Jews as extremists, or social media personalities exploiting them for views and clicks, the truth often becomes the first casualty. This phenomenon serves as a reminder of the importance of seeking accurate information from knowledgeable sources rather than relying on sensationalized media coverage.

The lesson learned from this experience is clear: in an age of instant global communication and viral social media, maintaining accuracy in religious reporting is more challenging – and more important – than ever. The story of the red heifers reminds us that ancient biblical traditions deserve careful, accurate reporting that respects their spiritual significance while avoiding political sensationalism and apocalyptic speculation.

CHAPTER SIXTEEN

Symbolism

T HE RED HEIFER is one of the most profound mysteries in biblical tradition. Jewish sages have long taught that the red heifer is a *chok* (divine mandate) considered the most enigmatic of all commandments. According to ancient Jewish tradition, even King Solomon, renowned as the wisest of all men, found himself unable to fully comprehend the deeper meaning of this commandment. This admission by such a towering figure of wisdom highlights this ritual's profound depth.

Yet, within its mysterious nature lies a powerful truth: sometimes, the greatest wisdom comes not from intellectual understanding but from faithful observance. The ancient Jewish text known as *Ethics of the Fathers* teaches that we cannot fully grasp the reasons behind God's commandments, nor can we know their ultimate rewards. This principle suggests that the true value of religious observance lies not in our comprehension but in our willingness to submit ourselves to divine wisdom.

The late Rabbi Jonathan Sacks, former Chief Rabbi of the United Hebrew Congregations of the Commonwealth, offered a profound perspective on this type of commandment. He explained that while non-Jews might readily understand Jewish laws based on social justice or historical memory, certain commands seem entirely irrational to outside observers. The Talmud itself acknowledges this, noting that such commandments were ones that "Satan and the nations of the world made fun of."

Rabbi Sacks argued that these seemingly irrational commandments fulfill a deeper purpose. The Hebrew word for these types of commands - *chok* - literally means 'to engrave,' suggesting something carved so deeply that it becomes permanent and indelible. These commands, he taught, were designed to bypass our rational mind - specifically the prefrontal cortex - and engage with something deeper within us. In the case of the red heifer, this might help explain its power to address our deepest fears about death and impurity in a way that pure logic never could.

"Faith from the world of *chok*, deeper than the rational mind – can help cure our deepest fears," Rabbi Sacks wrote. This insight helps us understand why such an apparently irrational ritual could have such a profound spiritual impact. It operates not at the level of intellect but at the level of soul.

Rabbi Binny Freedman, who heads the Orayta yeshiva near the site of the first two Temples in Jerusalem, has highlighted the contemporary relevance of this ancient ritual. "The red heifer is all about purifying those who came in contact with death, about re-engaging in life," he explains. This symbolism is especially relevant today, amid conflicts between cultures that glorify death and those that celebrate life.

Rabbi Freedman also points to another layer of symbolism: the Temple's role as a unifying force. "We see the Temple as a place where Jews come together to put aside their differences," he notes, adding that such unity "is also sorely needed right now." This observation highlights how the symbolism of the red heifer extends beyond individual purification to encompass broader themes of communal healing and reconciliation.

Rabbi Yosef Zvi Rimon, one of Israel's leading contemporary rabbinic authorities, sees in the red heifer a powerful symbol of

Jewish messianic hope and spiritual preparation. While examining the potential red heifers, he reflected on how their very appearance in our time serves as a profound reminder of the Jewish people's enduring faith in ultimate redemption. The emergence of red heifers in our generation symbolizes the continuous thread of hope and preparation that has sustained the Jewish people throughout history. This interpretation adds another layer to the red heifer's rich symbolism - beyond its role in purification from death, it becomes a living emblem of the Jewish people's constant spiritual vigilance and hope for the future.

The Jewish Sages have drawn attention to a fascinating connection between the red heifer and one of the most tragic episodes in biblical history - the sin of the Golden Calf. This event, which occurred just forty days after the divine revelation at Mount Sinai, marked a crucial turning point in human spiritual history. According to Jewish tradition, it was this sin that introduced the concept of death's impurity into the world.

To explain how the red heifer atones for the sin of the Golden Calf, the rabbis offer a powerful parable: "A handmaiden's son soiled the king's palace with his filth. The king commanded, 'Let the mother come, and clean up the child's filth'." In this analogy, the red heifer serves as the mother who comes to clean up the spiritual mess created by its "child" - the Golden Calf. This connection is reinforced through various details of the red heifer commandment.

For instance, the requirement that the heifer never have worn a yoke symbolically recalls how Israel "threw off the yoke of heaven" in worshiping the Golden Calf. The requirement for the heifer to be completely red connects to the biblical promise that "If your sins will be red as scarlet, they shall whiten as snow" (Isaiah 1:18). Yet it must be "perfect" in its redness, reminiscent of Israel's complete devotion to God before the sin.

On a personal level, the symbolism of the red heifer speaks

powerfully to the process of repentance and spiritual renewal. Many who have walked the path of religious return know the feeling of despair that can accompany serious sin. The weight of transgression can feel overwhelming, leading one to believe that true repentance is impossible. The Talmud teaches that a person sins only if a *ruach shtut* ("spirit of deviance") enters them, suggesting that sin represents a fundamental displacement of our true spiritual nature.

This is where the symbolism of immersion and purification becomes crucial. The ritual bath, or *mikveh*, plays a central role in Jewish practices of spiritual purification. As one rabbi poignantly observed, "How often do you jump into a hole in the ground and stop breathing?" This temporary suspension of breath, this moment of vulnerability and trust, becomes a powerful symbol of death and rebirth.

The red heifer ritual, with its complex procedures and mysterious power to purify those who have encountered death, represents this process of spiritual renewal on a profound level. The Prophet Ezekiel captured this transformative potential in his powerful words: "Then I shall sprinkle pure waters upon you, and you shall be clean, from all your uncleanness, and from all your idols, will I cleanse you. I will also give you a new heart, and I will place within you a new spirit..." (Ezekiel 36:25-26).

In our modern world, where rational explanation is often demanded for everything, the red heifer stands as a powerful reminder that some truths transcend human understanding. Its symbolism speaks to our deepest fears and highest hopes - our confrontation with mortality, our need for purification, our yearning for renewal, and our capacity for return to God. In all its mystery and enigma, it embodies the profound truth that sometimes the path to spiritual growth leads not through intellectual comprehension but through faithful observance and trust in divine wisdom.

Epilogue

Bat Ayin, Judea, 5885, 2125 CE

BAT AYIN WAS enveloped in the pre-dawn darkness, made even more impenetrable by the fogbank that rolled up the mountain from the coastal plain every night. The mist nurtured the terraced vineyards that dated back to the First Temple era, making Judean wine famous throughout the ancient world. But the fog made driving a slow affair, forcing Ephraim to wake up extra early for his journey to Jerusalem.

He made his way up the forest path, his long *peyot* and beard swaying in the cool morning air. The hills of Gush Etzion were silent except for his footsteps crackling on fallen leaves. He approached the ancient stone walls surrounding the natural spring that served as a ritual bath, disrobing quickly but pausing before jumping suddenly into the water. He surfaced, gasping as his lungs, shocked by the icy water, struggled to draw breath. He dressed quickly, struggling to focus on preparing for the day's special activities.

He walked home to find his sixteen-year-old daughter, Chana, waiting by his car, handing him a bagged lunch she had prepared. "Abba, I made you those sprouted grain crackers you like," she said. He stepped back into the house, grabbing the thermos of hot coffee he had prepared. The kitchen was filled with the aroma of the fresh-baked challah she was preparing for Shabbat.

Ephraim's electric car hummed quietly as he navigated Route 60, known locally as the Tunnel Road. He made a quick detour into Efrat to pick up his friend Shimon, a computer programmer who had made aliyah after the war. Shimon was scheduled to serve as a priest in the Temple, and his rotation was about to begin on the coming Sabbath. Shimon took his role as a priest quite seriously, but he preferred to get a ride to the Temple so he could leave the car with his wife for the entire week he was away.

While Ephraim drove, Shimon pulled out his phone and quickly navigated to the Third Temple's website. He signed in and checked for any last-minute changes at the Temple. He opened up the Yisrael section of the app.

"I'll order your turtledoves now," Shimon said, his fingers moving across the screen. "The system shows they have plenty available for today's voluntary offerings." In the trunk, Shimon's *bigdei kehuna* – the sacred garments of the priesthood – were carefully packed in a suitcase.

The massive underground parking complex beneath the Temple Mount was already filling with early morning visitors. Ephraim found a spot near the entrance to the new train station that connected the Temple complex to Ben Gurion Airport and Israel's rail network. After bidding farewell to Shimon, he made his way to the purification center. Seven days ago, he had taken his wife to the hospital for an ultrasound. While he waited, a message went out on the hospital's Whatsapp that a patient had passed away, rendering occupants of that wing of the hospital ritually impure. Three days later, a purification gathering was held in Gush Etzion, but Ephraim needed to be sprinkled again today, the seventh day, to bring his offering.

The red heifer complex combined modern efficiency with ancient tradition. Crowds moved through the tiled space in an orderly fashion as priests performed the sprinkling ritual. Afterward, Ephraim entered the adjoining facility with its heated ritual baths, reminiscent of an upscale health club but designed for ritual purification.

Ephraim exited, hurrying to the Western Wall Plaza, where he wrapped himself in his prayer shawl and put on his phylacteries for the morning service. As he concluded his prayers, a familiar voice called out. "Ephraim! Shalom, my friend!" Ephraim turned and smiled as he spotted his friend, Jim O'Donnell from Dallas, his characteristic Texas drawl carrying across the plaza.

They embraced warmly, remembering Ephraim's recent visit to Jim's church, where he had taught Torah classes. Jim wasn't alone – he had brought five other church members with him, all first-time visitors to Israel who wanted to offer Thanksgiving sacrifices.

The group gathered at the Western Wall, their voices joining in Psalm 66: "Come and see what God has done, His awesome deeds for mankind..." The massive LED screens above displayed the schedule of the daily sacrifices and the current Temple activities. Levitical music drifted through the speakers, accompanying the morning service.

When they reached the low stone boundary marking the inner Temple area, Jim and his group stopped. Ephraim continued alone, the coupons for all their offerings clutched in his hand while his Christian friends watched the proceedings on the large monitors. The morning sun now fully illuminated the gold-covered walls of the Third Temple, its splendor a testament to the fusion of ancient tradition and modern innovation.

We believe that Israel is the light to the nations and that the prophecies and promises are being fulfilled in its land faithfully. The Red Heifer is one of them and we are honored to support this book so the nations can be enlightened and blessed by it. We love and stand with Israel and we pray for the release of all the hostages and for the peace of Jerusalem.

We are thankful for Israel365, for the wonderful teachings and opportunities to demonstrate our love for Israel.

Angie & Dean Cole
West Virginia, USA

**IN APPRECIATION OF ISRAEL
AND HER PEOPLE,**
with our deepest love for God
and gratitude for His Word.
As the laws of the red heifer
are shared with the nations
through this book,we see a glimpse
of the prophet's vision:

*'Many nations shall come and say:
Come, let us go up to the
mountain of the LORD,
that He may teach us His ways,
and we may walk in His paths.'
—Micah 4:2*

May we soon see the complete
fulfillment of all His promises.

Patrizia and Rick Neel

In memory of

MARVIN DALE CAUSEY
(22.9.1942 - 29.11.2023)

and in honor of

CYNTHIA DALGO CAUSEY,

his beloved wife of 58 years.
Your unwavering love and support
have been a blessing to
your children.

With love,
Rebekah, David & Elisabeth

Sponsored by

Helen Ruth Davis

Laura Davis

Stand By Me

Hebrew Prayers for All Believers

Live Like David

Transform your daily spiritual practice with **Live Like David: Daily Devotional Journal,** an extraordinary three-volume masterwork that brings the timeless wisdom of King David into your daily life.

SCAN NOW!

Or visit israel365store.com

Bible Plus

By ISRAEL365

Study the Bible Like Never Before

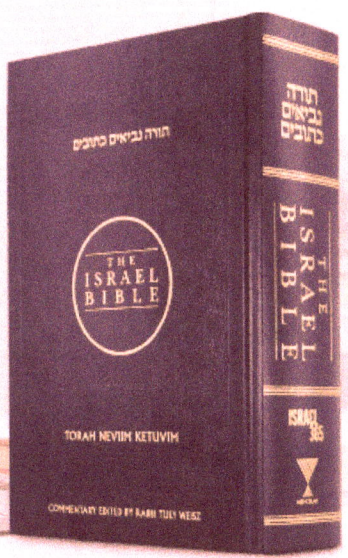

www.ingramcontent.com/pod-product-compliance
Lightning Source LLC
Chambersburg PA
CBHW071516120626
46550CB00006B/2240